AMERICAN AMERICAN WOMEN *of the* OLD WEST

Tricia Martineau Wagner

TWODOT®

GUILFORD, CONNECTICUT
HELENA, MONTANA
AN IMPRINT OF ROWMAN & LITTLEFIELD

A · T W O D O T® · B O O K

TwoDot is a registered trademark of Rowman & Littlefield
Distributed by NATIONAL BOOK NETWORK
Text design by M. A. Dubé
Front cover photo: Mary Fields, courtesy Sister Kathleen Padden of the Ursuline Convent Archives, Toledo, Ohio.
Back cover photos: Biddy Mason, courtesy Miriam Matthews Collection; Elizabeth Thorn Scott Flood, courtesy African American Museum and Library, Oakland (AAMLO); Mary Ellen Pleasant, courtesy San Francisco History Center, San Francisco Public Library, AAD-2997, from the Helen Holdredge Collection; and Annie Box Neal, courtesy Arizona Historical Society, Tucson, AH-22073.

Library of Congress Cataloging-in-Publishing Data
Wagner, Tricia Martineau.
    African American women of the Old West / Tricia Martineau Wagner.
    — 1st ed. p. cm.
    Includes bibliographical references and index.
    ISBN-13: 978-0-7627-3900-4

    1. African American women pioneers—West (U.S.)—Biography. 2. Women pioneers—West (U.S.)—Biography. 3. African Americans— West (U.S.)—Biography. 4. African American women pioneers—West (U.S.)—History. 5. Frontier and pioneer life—West (U.S.). 6. West (U.S.)—Biography. I. Title.
    E185.925.W34 2007
    305.48'896073078—dc22
    [B]   2006020774

Manufactured in the United States of America

For my father, Walter F. Martineau Jr.,

the greatest of storytellers,

thank you for showing me the way.

The woman who works on and on amid privations not only for herself but for her little ones and yet always sees victory ahead is the woman that not only makes husbands men in the true sense of the word, but who makes the men and women of tomorrow.

—H. R. Cayton

CONTENTS

ACKNOWLEDGMENTS

T HE TEN REMARKABLE WOMEN IN THIS BOOK
led lives that are worth remembering. Their stories were
buried in obscure sources and took a great deal of work to
unearth. I gratefully acknowledge the following people for their
assistance in the writing of this book:

- My editor, Erin E. Turner, at The Globe Pequot Press, whose
  expertise, professionalism, and encouragement helped turn
  my manuscript into a book. And to Kaleena Cote, whose guid-
  ance saw the manuscript through its final stages. Thank you.

- Esther Hall Mumford and Dr. Quintard Taylor, historians and
  authors, for pointing me in the right direction when I began
  my research.

- Beth R. Olsen, historian, researcher, and dear friend, for all her
  research efforts; especially for uncovering a plethora of material on Jane Manning James and for her clarification of LDS
  terminology. Her support and inspiration are immeasurable.

- Sister Kathleen Padden, OSU Toledo and the Archives at St.
  Ursula Convent Toledo, Ohio, for her generous assistance with
  research materials on Mary Fields. Her love shines through as
  brightly now as it did when she was my high school principal at
  St. Ursula Academy in Toledo.

- Irene Mahoney, OSU College of New Rochelle, for willingly
  sharing her research on Mary Fields and Mother Amadeus in
  the writing of her book *Lady Blackrobes*.

- Francis Xavier Porter, OSU Ursuline Archives, Great Falls,
  Montana, for searching out material on Mary Fields.

- Anne-Marie Rachman, Michigan State University Library, Special Collections, whose excellence in research enabled me to write the chapter on Abby Fisher.

- Erika Schmidt, reference/cataloging librarian, Mechanics' Institute Library, San Francisco, for her research assistance with Abby Fisher.

- Wallace De Young and Beverly K. Smith of Wells Fargo, for their assistance with the research on Mary Fields. And Dr. Andy Anderson, Wells Fargo chief historian, for sharing his online genealogy research information.

- Jacqueline E. A. Lawson, Black Heritage Society of Washington State Inc., for setting me up with several researchers and contacts.

- Susan Bragg, PhD, History Department, University of Washington, for her research assistance and direction.

- Betty Marvin, Oakland Cultural Heritage Survey, Oakland, California, City Planning Department, for her research assistance with Elizabeth Thorn Scott Flood.

- Peter Berg, assistant director for special collections, Michigan State University, for his research assistance with Abby Fisher.

- Dr. Louis H. Bronson, for his research assistance with Elizabeth Thorn Scott Flood and the history of St. Andrew's AME Church, Sacramento.

- Veronica Lee, research librarian for the African-American Museum and Library in Oakland (AAMLO), for her research assistance with Elizabeth Thorn Scott Flood, Biddy Mason, and Mary Ellen Pleasant.

- Ross Sutherland, archivist at the Marion County Historical Society, Salem, Oregon, for his research assistance with Mary Jane Holmes Shipley Drake.

- Ellen M. Shea, head of public services, Schlesinger Library on the History of Women in America, Radcliffe Institute for Advanced Study, Harvard University, for the direction offered in researching Abby Fisher.

- Rev. Dr. Richard Evans of Colorado, for his research assistance with Clara Brown.

- Tom Thompson, coordinator of the Acadia Ranch Museum of the Oracle Historical Society, Arizona, for his research assistance with Annie Neal.

- William Nation, research librarian at the Morrison Branch of the Public Library of Charlotte & Mecklenburg County, for his instruction on researching online resources.

- Peter Jareo, library supervisor of the Carmel Branch of the Public Library of Charlotte & Mecklenburg County and his staff, for cheerfully processing the seemingly endless requests for interlibrary loan materials.

- The friends and members of my book club, who kindly assisted with retrieving a multitude of books for my research: Carolyn Bremer, Betsy Day, Pat Dorcy, Susie Hensler, Amy Norman, Sherry Williams, and Beth Wright.

- Walter Martineau and Lois Holmes, for diligently collecting antiques and artifacts for my school presentations and for their encouragement in the writing of this book.

- Joan Rush, ny research assistant and friend, whose sense of humor keeps me going.

- My husband and best friend, Mark, who is always there for me, and our children, Kelsey and Mitch, for complimenting me, saying, "For Mom and her book." All my love is yours.

INTRODUCTION

GENERATIONS OF AMERICANS HAVE READ HISTORY books describing the exploits of the men—almost always the white men—who settled the West. What about the women? They were there, too. A national history written solely about the contributions of women that purported to tell the whole story while excluding the accomplishments of men would of course be ludicrous. Yet for the most part, historians have ignored the contributions and achievements women have made, especially women of color.

The brave pioneers who went ahead to make life easier for those who followed in their footsteps were not always male, and they were not always white. It took a combined effort to make a life on the frontier. A lot of "sweat equity" went into building a house, making a living, and creating a community that had some semblance of civility. Early towns would not grow until schools, churches, and other organizations were established to foster a sense of community, and those were often started by women.

That women have been underrepresented in our nation's history is an understatement. That black women have been doubly overlooked for so long is a shame. African American women *were* on the western frontier, albeit in far smaller numbers than most other groups, but they were there. Unfortunately, very few people thought their lives, their struggles, and their accomplishments were important enough to record. The lives of African American women and their achievements must be reconstructed from public records such as marriage, birth, and death certificates, census reports, deeds, and from old newspaper accounts and other archival sources, including oral histories that have been committed to paper, reminiscences, and personal journals and diaries. The pieces of the puzzle are waiting to be put together. Our invisible sisters whisper their stories to us; they are just waiting to be told.

The ten remarkable women in *African American Women of the Old West* are individuals all born before 1900. None of them knew one another. Some were slaves, some were free, and some had been both. They settled in California, Oregon, Washington, Colorado, Montana, Utah, and Arizona. They were laundresses, freedom advocates, entrepreneurs, journalists, educators, midwives, business proprietors, religious converts, philanthropists, mail and freight haulers, and civil and social activists. Their lives were not insignificant.

They overcame incredible odds in the face of discrimination and ostracism, bearing witness to the importance of believing in oneself. None of the women expected the world to hand her anything other than a fair chance—and when it didn't do that much, they did not sit back and take it. These women found a way to live outside the parameters that society had set for them. They went west to free themselves from such constraints. Still, prejudicial attitudes permeated policies that restricted their lives. The West offered economic independence and professional opportunities for upwardly mobile black women. Yet, making their way in the West was still far from easy, and they struggled to survive. They were ordinary women who led remarkable lives despite the odds against them.

The importance of women in major movements in history, especially in regional settlement and development, cannot be underestimated. It was through these women's hard work and perseverance that change was brought about. Their unrelenting determination to succeed opened the doors of opportunity for those following behind them. They realized that general uplift of their race would be accomplished through education, church involvement, and community outreach. They formed social groups and clubs not just for entertainment and support, but also to reform and refine their society.

The best part of writing about the women in this book was the chance to bring them back to life; to validate that their lives did indeed matter. Let us look to these women for their strength, admire them for their courage, and emulate them to make the world a better place. Though they never looked for recognition, their accomplishments should not go unnoticed.

The account of black women in history is like an old patch-work quilt with missing threads and holes: a story incomplete in its details, yet treasured for what it once was. Let us listen to the hushed voices of our sisters so that their stories are not lost forever. The fabric of their lives needs to be woven into the tapestry of our nation's history.

THE OPEN HAND

Biddy Mason

EIGHTEEN-YEAR-OLD BIDDY MASON HAD NO idea that her life was about to change on that oppressively hot day in 1836. But when her master, John Smithson, came bounding into the house unexpectedly, everyone knew something was up. For days the slaves in the main house had been ordered to clean endlessly and hurriedly, without knowing the purpose of such urgency. Perhaps the time had come for the mystery to be unveiled.

Master Smithson singled out Biddy and called her away from her morning chores, even though she was only halfway through. Practically giddy with excitement, Smithson eagerly told her to be bathed, dressed in her finest clothes, and ready and waiting when he called. Biddy was glad to be excused from her work and obediently followed his directive to make herself look presentable and be cheerful. It was not her place to ask why.

Later that afternoon Biddy was summoned. She was as fresh as the spring air, her hair was perfectly plaited, and she wore the plain new dress laid out especially for her. She picked up a small magnolia blossom and put it behind her ear as she walked to the main house. She stood silently next to John Smithson on the grand wraparound porch of his South Carolina plantation in full anticipation.

Following her master's gaze, Biddy noticed some movement on the horizon, and her heart began to flutter. A fancy carriage soon emerged from a dust cloud that was making its way up the tree-lined dirt road. When the carriage came to a halt in front of the estate, out stepped the newly married and splendidly attired Mr. and Mrs. Robert Marion Smith.

Biddy stepped respectfully off to the side while the guests were being enthusiastically received. Then Master Smithson, barely able to contain his excitement, presented his dear cousin, the bride Rebecca, with her wedding present. "Here!" he announced, thrusting Biddy toward the new bride. At once it occurred to Biddy that this was the moment at which she was to "look presentable and be cheerful." Though her heart sank, she forced a smile onto her face and bent her head politely. Then she noticed that her magnolia blossom had fallen to the ground and lay trampled next to her bare feet. Just like that, she had been given away.

The Smiths would be the fourth family who had owned Biddy, and she was not yet in her twenties. Perhaps the emotional upheaval that this last transaction had put her on was a defining moment in young Bridget Mason's life. She vowed then and there that if she could help it, she would never allow anyone to be treated like a piece of property again. No matter how poor people were, Biddy felt, they should be allowed their dignity.

Two other house servants were included as part of the wedding gift to Mr. and Mrs. Smith: Hannah, who was Biddy's sister, and another female slave named Ella. Additionally, a blacksmith named Buck was to accompany them to serve Mr. Smith.

There was not much time for good-byes, and after the wedding celebration was over, the slaves packed up their meager

Biddy Mason
COURTESY MIRIAM MATTHEWS COLLECTION

belongings and were on their way. For the next eight years, they would live with the Smiths in Logtown, Mississippi.

Biddy's responsibilities were to oversee the household and to personally attend to the mistress, Mrs. Smith. This occupied much of her time, as Mrs. Smith was often in poor health. Biddy's early training as a midwife also kept her quite busy over the years. There was no shortage of heirs for Master Smith. He would have six children by his wife, Rebecca; nine by Biddy's sister, Hannah; and three by Biddy herself.

Biddy probably would have lived out her life in Mississippi had not the Smiths come in contact with members of the Church of Latter-day Saints. When the Smiths converted to the Mormon faith in 1844, her life went in a direction she could never have imagined. Robert Smith decided to take his family and join up with fellow believers who were establishing Mormon communities out West. Biddy found herself moving once again, this time 1,700 miles across the country to the Utah Territory. Thus she unwillingly became part of a religious pilgrimage that was connected to neither her race nor her faith.

Three other families banded together with the Smiths for the cross-country journey: the Bankses of Georgia, the Crosbys of Mississippi, and the Smithsons of South Carolina. Biddy knew the families well, for she had been previously owned by each of them. Now she was to be a servant for all the families as the close band of friends trekked westward. Together they were part of a three-hundred-wagon caravan that set out over the Oregon/Mormon Trail. They left Fulton, Mississippi, on March 10, 1848. Thirty-four slaves and fifty-six whites were among the entourage walking from Mississippi to Utah. Smith's party was comprised of almost equal numbers of slaves and white people.

The seven-month journey was an exhausting one. Thirty-year-old Biddy had to carry her infant daughter, Harriet, whom she was nursing, as well as care for her older children, Ellen and Ann (aged ten and four), in addition to carrying out her chores. Besides cooking the daily meals, Biddy's responsibilities included setting up and breaking camp each day, herding the cattle and livestock through the choking dust at the end of the wagon train, and putting her skills as a midwife to use.

The "Mississippi Saints," as the Mormon travelers were called, survived the arduous cross-country trek. They settled with their slaves in the Holladay-Cottonwood area of the Salt Lake Valley.

There the fledgling community comprised 1,700 people, with the ratio of whites to blacks being 330:1. There had been talk of the slaves attaining their freedom when they reached their destination in Utah. Though such wishful thinking may have spurred Biddy on, emancipation never occurred. They all remained in servitude with the Smiths for another three years in Utah.

However, a request from the Mormon Church to its followers in 1851 changed Biddy Mason's fate. Brigham Young, the church leader, was looking for volunteers to establish a Mormon settlement in California. The church wanted to set up a way station for Mormon pilgrims sailing around South America to California and then continuing on to Utah. Biddy's master, Robert Smith, recently converted, received the idea most enthusiastically. He decided to go to California and take his slaves with him.

The previous year, in 1850, California had been admitted to the Union as a free state. That fact did not worry Robert Smith, even though Brigham Young had cautioned those followers who still held slaves about it, saying: "There is little doubt but [the slaves] will all be free as soon as they arrive in California." Instead Smith confidently headed west once again, taking his household and his servants with him in oxcarts. It apparently never occurred to him that his slave ownership would be challenged—or perhaps he arrogantly assumed that no court would rule in favor of a slave.

Smith's 150-wagon caravan left Utah's Great Salt Basin and followed the path of the California Trail heading for San Bernardino County, California. Thirty-three-year-old Biddy and her sister, Hannah, came in contact with new people and radical ideas in the various campgrounds along the way, meeting a number of free blacks. The ideas of Charles H. and Elizabeth (Flake) Rowan in particular opened up a world of possibilities to

Biddy. The Rowans encouraged Biddy and her extended family to contest their slave status upon entering California. A glimmer of hope burned within Biddy's heart for the first time.

During the five years that Biddy, Hannah, and their eleven children lived with the Smiths in San Bernardino, Robert Smith disregarded the fact that slavery was illegal in California. Biddy and her family made many new friends and acquaintances, and of all the people they met, the Owens family was the most important and influential. Robert and Minnie Owens were ex-slaves who ran a successful corral. They were financially independent free blacks who had hired *vaqueros,* or Mexican cowboys, to work as hands on their ranch. Their free status bolstered Biddy's resolve to seek her freedom. Popular opinion against slavery was increasing, and when Biddy met other antislavery activists, they further encouraged her to take action. Still, she held back, waiting for the right opportunity.

The Owens family had become fond of Biddy, and by 1855 their children had become romantically involved. Biddy's seventeen-year-old daughter, Ellen, had fallen in love with the Owenses' son, Charles. Hannah's daughter, Ann, had fallen love with Manuel Pepper, one of the *vaqueros* who worked for the Owens family. These relationships fortuitously cemented the families together. When it was rumored that Robert Smith was thinking of moving to Texas, taking the Masons with him so that he could keep them as his slaves, the Owens family took an interest. No one wanted to see the Masons leave the area. It became apparent that something needed to be done quickly when Smith gathered up his belongings, slaves included, and started his trek toward Texas.

In December 1855 Robert Smith decided to stop with his caravan in Los Angeles before heading for Texas. Their wagon train camped in Cajon Pass for three months while plans for the new settlement in Texas were drawn up. They were also awaiting the birth of Hannah Smith's ninth baby.

During their stopover Biddy met additional members of Los Angeles' black community who also encouraged them to seek their freedom. Now that the Masons had the support of the Owenses, and their *vaqueros,* if needed, this was their prime opportunity to press for their freedom.

Charles and Elizabeth Rowan, whom Biddy had met on the trek to California four years earlier, joined forces with the Owenses. Young Charles Owens and his father and other members of the two families, along with the *vaqueros,* formed a posse and set off like knights in shining armor from their livery on San Pedro Street in Los Angeles. Riding into the Smiths' camp near Santa Monica, the group apprehended Smith's wagon train, preventing it from leaving the state. They had been wise to get the law on their side.

The Los Angeles county sheriff, Frank Dewitt, had been informed that Robert Smith was intent upon taking his slaves to Texas, a slave state, in an attempt to hold on to his property. Judge Benjamin Hayes was petitioned, and a writ of habeas corpus was issued against Smith forbidding him to leave the state. The slaves were placed "under the charge of the sheriff for their protection" and were housed in the county jail so that no one could abscond with them.

On January 19, 1856, Biddy Mason, who was illiterate, formally petitioned the court for freedom for herself, her three daughters, and her extended family of thirteen other slaves belonging to Smith. Robert Smith claimed that he was the slaves' legal guardian and that some of the slaves were willing to go to

Texas with him. In spite of California's free-state status, the odds were against Biddy and her family. California law prohibited minorities such as blacks, mulattos, Chinese, and Native Americans from testifying against white people.

Smith attempted to take two of the slave children to Texas secretly while the case was still being heard. Biddy Mason's attorney, who was offered a bribe by Smith's attorney, quit during the trial. It is also believed that Robert Smith may have made threats to both Hannah and Biddy. All this may have hurt Smith's case in the end.

District court Judge Benjamin Hayes heard the case for three days before handing down his ruling. During that time the Masons' hopes rose and fell like the waves on the ocean. Life could be difficult if they were forced to return to a master whom they had challenged. Without protection from the law, they could be whipped—or worse.

In the end Judge Hayes's decision upheld the state's 1849 constitution, which created California as a free state. He found that "all men should be left to their own pursuit of freedom and happiness." Biddy Mason probably could not believe her ears when she heard the words from the judge's mouth: "All of the said persons of color are entitled to their freedom and are free forever."

A jubilant Biddy Mason and her family left the courtroom on January 21, 1856, as free people. Their life of servitude was finally over. Judge Hayes placed thirty-eight-year-old Biddy and her relatives under the protective custody of Sheriff Burnside, and Smith reportedly left town without paying the court costs as he had been ordered to do.

Biddy Mason took full advantage of the chance to earn her own money and make her own way in life with her newfound free status. She found California to be a land of opportunity despite the discrimination encountered by minorities. Settling in Los Angeles, the Masons temporarily moved in with the Owens family until they could afford a place of their own. Charles Owens claimed his bride, Ellen Mason, and they were wed.

Relying on skills she had honed all her life—herbal medicine, midwifery, and nursing—Biddy Mason found employment with Dr. John S. Griffin on Main Street as both a nurse and midwife. For more than a quarter century, she served the surrounding communities using her skills. She brought hundreds of children of all classes into the world. She also worked as a nurse at the county's jail and hospital.

Mason saved her daily wages of $2.50 for ten years. Then she made one of the best decisions of her life—she invested in real estate. On November 28, 1866, Mason became one of the first black female landowners in Los Angeles. The acquisition of property was the way to ensure financial independence for her family. She purchased two lots between Spring Street and Fort (Broadway) between Third and Fourth Streets for $250. Part of the land she kept vacant; it is thought she built some small rental units on another section. Meanwhile she rented a small place on San Pedro Street to live in.

Mason was also a strong community leader. She and her son-in-law, Charles Owens, helped found the First African Methodist Episcopal Church, Los Angeles's first black church. Biddy's small home on San Pedro Street served as a meeting place for the fledgling congregation in 1872 until a church was built.

Biddy's lack of a formal education did not prevent her from succeeding. Her wise real estate transactions made her a fortune. Her property was a prime location and became the city center, which would later become the heart of Los Angeles's financial district. She built a commercial two-story brick building on another piece of property at 331 Spring Street, leasing storage rooms in the lower half and residing in the upper half.

In 1884 Mason sold a parcel of her properties for $1,500 and another for $44,000. As the town of Los Angeles expanded, the value of her land acquisitions grew accordingly. Soon she had amassed the staggering fortune of $300,000.

Attaining legendary status, "Grandma Mason" was known for her generosity to others. Quoted as saying, "Greet the world with an open hand," she never turned down anyone in need, regardless of race or creed. Her home was referred to as the "House of the Open Hand." Biddy Mason reportedly nursed people stricken with the highly contagious smallpox and took her home-cooked meals to inmates in jail. She donated land for schools, hospitals, and churches. She opened a nursery and care center for black children of working parents. She supported various charities and contributed to worthwhile social causes in her community. In the 1880s, when a flood left many of the townspeople homeless, Biddy set up an open account for flood victims at the local grocery store.

Biddy was immensely proud to see her children and grand-children educated and successful. She made sure that her daughters were educated—education brought respect. Biddy's eldest daughter, Ellen, had married Charles Owens after completing her education. Ellen and Charles sent their children to the public school in Oakland, California (where Charles ran a successful livery stable) and then to business school.

In 1885 Biddy offered a portion of the land upon which her home was built to her grandsons, Robert and Henry Owens, who built a livery stable there that served the city of Los Angeles, which by then had a population of more than 50,000, including more than 1,200 blacks. Her grandson, Robert Curry Owens, went on to become a real estate developer, a politician, and eventually one of Los Angeles's wealthiest African Americans.

When Biddy died, the *Los Angeles Times* summed up her life in her obituary: "Biddy Mason died January 15, 1891, at the age of 73, after 40 years of good works." She was buried in an unmarked grave in the Evergreen Cemetery in the Boyle Heights area of Los Angeles.

The Spring Street area, where Biddy purchased her first two parcels of land, remained the financial district of Los Angeles until the 1920s. By the time the financial district relocated to Bunker Hill and the Figueroa Corridor in the 1960s, however, all evidence of Mason's home was lost.

The Community Redevelopment Agency (CRA) of Los Angeles attempted to revitalize Spring Street by bringing a sizable state office building to the site years later. It was not until a ten-story parking garage was being built to accompany the Broadway-Spring Shopping Center there that evidence of Biddy Mason's life resurfaced. Artifacts from her homestead were uncovered during demolition of the property located between Spring Street and Broadway at Third Street.

The CRA asked the Power of Place to recognize Biddy Mason. Power of Place was a nonprofit organization committed to honoring the memory of early Angelenos who made significant contributions to society—and especially to celebrate the works of women and minorities important in Los Angeles's urban history. It was decided that some form of public art would best commemorate the life of Biddy Mason.

Ninety-seven years after her death, members of the First African Methodist Episcopal Church, which she had helped found, provided Mason with the proper recognition. They organized to lay a tombstone on her grave on March 27, 1988. In attendance were 3,000 members of the congregation; the mayor of Los Angeles, Tom Bradley; and two of Biddy Mason's descendants.

November 16, 1989, was declared Biddy Mason Day, and there between Spring Street and Broadway at Third Street, on property known as Biddy Mason Park the commissioned pieces of art were unveiled. Artists had collaborated on interpretive pieces, making the most of their limited space. The artworks are located in pedestrian walkways between buildings as well as in the small adjacent park area. Permanent photographic murals, plaques, embossed images, and artifacts chronicle her life. The elevator lobby of the parking garage boasts an 8- by 81-foot concrete wall. Embossed into the wall are three-dimensional images representative of Biddy Mason: a midwife's bag, a wagon wheel, her freedom papers, and the deed to her property.

Those who pass through this elevator lobby can pause to appreciate her accomplishments. Rising from her humble beginnings in slavery, Bridget Mason—a single mother and head of a large extended household—led her family on cross-country journeys. She bravely sought their freedom, provided for her children and descendants, and opened her heart to anyone in need. Biddy Mason became a driving force in Los Angeles's African American community. Her extraordinary social activism, based in her long-held belief in the worth of every individual, fulfilled the promise she had made to herself long before as a young woman.

A Force to Be
Dealt With
Mary Fields

THE ROUGH-AND-READY FRONTIER MEN WHO frequented the saloons in Cascade, Montana, in the early 1900s thought they'd seen it all, but they were mistaken. One minute they were busy playing cards and drinking shots of whiskey, and the next their game was interrupted. Without warning Mary Fields pushed back her chair and angrily threw her hand across the table. She bit down hard on the cigar hanging from the side of her mouth, her eyes slowly following a figure passing by the window of her favorite drinking establishment. As Mary stood up, her seething temper rose even higher.

The lively bar music came to a halt as the buxom, 6-foot-tall, 200-pound, 70-something Negro laundress stomped out of the Silver Dollar Saloon. She had apparently recognized someone walking by the window and determinedly went out after him. Catching up with the man, who had skipped town without paying his $2.00 laundry bill, she spun him around and punched him with her iron fist. Wiping her hands on her apron, she went back into the saloon and declared that the gentleman's bill "was now paid in full." The music resumed, as did the card game, to the howls of laughter from the other players, who shook their heads at the stupidity of anyone who messed with Mary Fields. Who would go up against the only woman granted permission by Mayor D. W. "Bill" Munroe to drink in Cascade's saloons—a privilege reserved otherwise solely for men? Anybody foolish enough to take advantage of this whiskey-drinking, cigar-smoking, gun-toting man of a woman clearly deserved whatever he got.

Mary Fields was born a slave on a plantation in Hickman County, Tennessee, around 1832. Her sheer size and contentious nature had most assuredly set her apart at an early age. Fully capable of doing a man's work, she likely spent a great deal of time working alongside the males. This may have played a part in her fiercely independent nature, indomitable spirit, and fearlessness. These strong personality traits defined who she was and how she lived. Mary Fields's life is a study in contrasts, in opposites attracting, and in opposing forces colliding, all of which no doubt contribute to the contradictory accounts of a woman who became a legend in her own time.

There are conflicting versions of the story of Mary's early years. It is not known exactly how she became acquainted with the young woman who would change the course of her life: Miss Sarah Theresa Dunne, later to become Mother Mary Amadeus, a Roman Catholic Ursuline nun. The two women, separated in age by fourteen years, were as different as night and day. Miss Dunne was born on July 2, 1846, in Akron, Ohio. Mary Fields never knew her own birthdate and estimated the year to be 1832. Sarah Dunne had a fair complexion and blond hair and blue eyes and was descended from a wealthy Irish family. Mary was dark skinned with black hair and dark eyes, the child of slave parents. Sarah was frail and delicate; Mary was strong and sturdy. Sarah was educated early in life; Mary became literate only years later. Sarah was refined and patient; Mary was rough and quick

Mary Fields
COURTESY SISTER KATHLEEN PADDEN OF THE
URSULINE CONVENT ARCHIVES, TOLEDO, OHIO

tempered. But the two seemed to have an affinity for each other that would last a lifetime.

Some accounts say that Mary Fields worked for the Dunne family when Sarah was a child, but others say that the Dunnes never owned slaves. Mary Fields may have first met Sarah Dunne while Mary was a servant for Franklin Warner, a Tennessee plantation owner and friend of the Dunnes. At some point their paths did cross, but surely neither woman realized the bond that would develop between them.

After the passage of the Thirteenth Amendment, which formally freed the slaves in 1865, Mary Fields found herself a free woman at the age of about thirty-three. Five years later, she had found employment emptying chamber pots on the *Robert E. Lee,* a prominent steamboat running on the Mississippi River. Mary loved to tell the story of being a part of the renowned race between two of the great steamboats of the time, the *Lee* and the steamboat *Natchez.* The three-day race from New Orleans to St. Louis—held June 30 to July 2, 1870—was of national interest, with towns telegraphing the race times as the steamships raced up the Mississippi at an average of 14 miles per hour. White steam reportedly spouted from the pipes and black steam from the chimneys as every rivet in the boilers was strained. Sparks filled the sky as the coal-fueled *Natchez* took on the wood-fueled *Lee.* Mary relayed how anything and everything was thrown into the fire to produce enough steam to win—resin, bacon, and even whole sides of ham. It's not hard to envision Mary stoking the fires herself and jubilantly celebrating her ship's well-earned victory over the *Natchez* in just three days, eighteen hours, and fourteen minutes—a full six hours and thirty-six minutes ahead.

It may have been while on the *Robert E. Lee* that Mary Fields became reacquainted with Miss Sarah Dunne's older brother, who was by then Judge Edmond Dunne. Mary Fields became employed as a confidential servant for Judge and Mrs. Dunne for several years.

Both Judge Dunne and his wife had sisters who had become Ursuline nuns. They lived at the Ursuline Catholic Convent in Toledo, Ohio, where Miss Sarah Dunne and Miss Mary Raphael Warner were known as Sister Mary Amadeus and Sister Annunciation, respectively. This knowledge may have influenced Mary's decision to make her way to Toledo eventually. Perhaps Mary Fields was seeking out the only family she felt she had when looking for her next employment situation.

Fortunately the good sisters at the Ursuline Convent of the Sacred Heart, located on Cherry and Erie Streets in Toledo, took Mary in. There she dedicated herself to the Ursuline sisters from the late 1870s to the mid-1880s. She was given a room on the first floor of the convent and had her own kneeler at the back of the chapel. "Black Mary," as she was called, always dressed in black— wearing a black apron over her black dress (some say over men's pants) and donning a black skullcap. Along with her extraordinary height and great bearing, this gave her a rather imposing appearance, especially with a cigar dangling from the crook of her mouth. Mary planted the garden, tended the cloister courtyard, and took great pride in keeping up the grounds. She kept a watchful eye on the schoolchildren at the convent to see that no one disturbed her well-manicured lawn. The schoolgirls were said to be frightened of Black Mary's gruff manner and quick temper. As one nun remarked, "God help anyone who walked on the lawn after Mary had cut it." Mary Fields was a hard worker and she was proud of being largely self-sufficient. Her wages were $50 per year, out of which she paid for all of her incidental expenses, such as her traveling bag, musical instruments, and medical prescriptions.

Though she was dedicated to her work, Mary enjoyed relaxation with her pet dog and her music: She had her own banjo and harmonica. Come Election Day, Mary could be seen riding around town with wild abandon, smoking a cigar, and campaigning vigorously for her candidate.

Sister Amadeus and Mary Fields became very fond of each other, and it must have saddened Mary, then, to see Sister Amadeus contemplating leaving the convent to go out West. In 1880 Bishop John T. Brondel of Vancouver, who was also in charge of the Montana Territory, contacted the Ursuline sisters in Toledo. Jesuit missionaries in the West needed the Ursuline sisters' assistance to carry on the work they had been doing there. For nearly twenty years they had been setting up relief centers and Indian missions for Native Americans. Bishop Brondel asked the Ursuline sisters to institute educational programs and to operate the western missions. They were to open boarding schools for children of both white pioneers and Blackfoot Indians. Thirty sisters answered the bishop's call for assistance as missionaries; six were chosen, Sister Amadeus among them. Sister Amadeus was promoted to Mother Superior, and in 1884 the six nuns found themselves on the long journey west—1,600 miles to the Montana Territory.

The frontier had been inching ever westward, pushing bands of Indian tribes into other Indians' land. In addition to the bloody territorial disputes they had been through, the displaced Natives faced starvation as their buffalo were slaughtered by settlers. They were defenseless against foreign strains of diseases that they had no immunity to. Additionally, alcoholism was a growing problem among the Indians. The sisters recognized the desperate plight of the Native Americans and were there to set up relief centers at the missions. They wished to bring Native peoples hope by bringing them closer to God.

The Ursuline sisters did not realize just how primitive the conditions they were facing were when they pulled into Miles City, Montana, after their three-day train trip. The temperature was forty degrees below zero. The town, designated as a supply station for nearby Fort Keogh, boasted sixty-five saloons yet had little else in the way of civilized society. The nuns toiled incessantly to establish a much-needed boarding school for pioneer children. They also worked to establish a mission among the Cheyenne, Crow, Blackfoot, and Gros Ventre–Assiniboine Indian reservations located in central and eastern Montana, an area 14 miles northwest of Cascade. A generous offer of financial assistance from the Jesuits, along with a farm, a few wagons and cows, and $220 worth of provisions, enticed the sisters to establish an extension at St. Peter's Mission in late October 1884.

By 1885 the Jesuit priests began turning St. Peter's Mission over to the Ursuline nuns. In April 1885, however, Mother Amadeus became ill with pneumonia. Months of sleeping on the cabin floor through cold winters and wet springs added to the stress of being undernourished and overworked. When word of her illness reached the Toledo convent, nothing could prevent the fifty-three-year-old Mary Fields from accompanying Mother Stanislaus to Montana to nurse Mother Amadeus back to health.

Once in Montana, Mary refused to leave Mother Amadeus while she was ill. Afterward Mary insisted on staying on at St.

Peter's Mission—and that was final. She, too, would brave the harsh Montana winters while living in log cabins, as long as she could be near her beloved friend again.

For eight years Mary assisted with the building of the Ursuline sisters' stone convent nestled in the foothills of the mountains, 19 miles from the town of Cascade (formally called Dodge). Mary, who answered to no one, insisted on earning her keep. She did much of the hard labor herself, hauling building materials of stone and lumber from the wagon to the site. Hard work was no stranger to Mary Fields, and she was more than willing to tackle any task. Yet she was quick to get her ire up and readily took on any of the hired hands if provoked.

Besides construction of the mission's three stone buildings and the wooden church, her jobs included doing the laundry, tending the garden, raising chickens, handling any odd jobs, and preparing the chapel altar for Mass. Mary also drove the freight wagon through all kinds of adverse weather, faithfully delivering food and supplies to the mission. While Mary preferred to settle her arguments with her fists, it was well known that she carried a .38-caliber Smith & Wesson pistol under her apron for protection when she drove the freight wagon. This single-action firearm could be easily stashed and was perfect for close work. It was said that Mary "couldn't miss a thing within fifty paces." Reliable as she was, she saw her deliveries through and would take on anyone who dared to prevent her from doing so.

Mary was not easily intimidated, and her temper got her into many altercations, verbal and physical. The combination of her coarse language, affinity for liquor and cigars, and explosive disposition earned her a reputation as the "terror of the countryside." She once gave a pelting of rocks to a man who'd insulted her verbally. Another altercation in 1894 with a hired hand led to a duel in which Mary's bullet came close enough to the offender that he learned not to mess with her again. Reports of such incidents reached Bishop Brondel's ears, which concerned him, for it did not put the mission in a favorable light. When news of the shootout reached him in Helena, he decided he'd heard enough. The Native American girls were being taught nineteenth-century Victorian customs and manners so as to fit into fine society. There was no place for a showdown at a mission school. The bishop insisted that Mary Fields be directed to leave the mission permanently, and not even Mary herself could dissuade him. After nearly ten years of unswerving devotion to the Ursuline nuns, Mary packed her bags. To the sisters' great dismay, this directive not only separated Mary from them, but estranged her from the church as well.

Mother Amadeus saw to it that Mary Fields was not far away, though. She was set up in the restaurant business in nearby Cascade. At age sixty-two Mary Fields began her brief career as a restaurateur. Underneath her rough exterior, her heart was as big as the Montana Territory. She ended up giving away far too many meals, especially to poor local sheepherders. Her continual benevolence toward those who were hungry and the credit she extended to her nonpaying customers were of course admirable, but her business failed. Refusing food to no one, she went broke not once, but twice.

Perhaps Mother Amadeus thought it best to concentrate on Mary's skills to find her employment. At sixty-four Mary still feared no one. She was aggressive and could expertly handle two teams of horses better than any man around. Therefore the Mother Superior managed to secure a job for which Mary was well qualified—driver for the U.S. mail. In fact Mary's route was between Cascade and St. Peter's Mission, and this enabled her to see her friend and the other sisters on a regular basis.

Thus she became the second female mail carrier in the country. At this Mary excelled. Many took her for a man with the dark clothing, skullcap, and man's overcoat that she wore. Seated atop the stagecoach, she would hold the reins, crack the whip, and drive her team triumphantly into the mission, jolting wildly on the spring suspension that nearly catapulted her from her high perch. Everyone knew when the mail or passengers had arrived from Cascade. With jug of whiskey by her foot, a pistol packed under her apron, and a shotgun by her side, "Stagecoach Mary," as she came to be called, was ready to take on any aggressor. The shotgun she toted was one of the most feared of guns. It could cut a man in two at short range, and Mary wouldn't hesitate to do so.

For eight years Mary carried mail on her 19-mile route. She was a swift and reliable courier, as dedicated an employee as there ever was. Not once did she miss a day's work. No rainstorm, snowstorm, or forty-below weather stopped her. Often she slept in the train terminal awaiting a delivery. Once when her wagon was stranded in a Montana blizzard, she got down and paced the whole night, refusing to allow herself to freeze to death. If other weather extremes forced her to abandon her stagecoach, she strapped the mail bag over her broad shoulders and walked back to the mission.

While she was en route one day, a pack of wolves frightened the horses, and the stagecoach overturned. Mary held vigil all night, keeping the hungry wolves at bay with her pistol and shotgun. At daybreak she was found alive, the mission's supplies intact. Unconventional as she was, Mary obviously took her sworn oath to protect the U.S. mail very seriously. She wasn't the least bit bothered by the long hours and low pay.

Mary suffered just one accident in all her years: She was thrown from the stagecoach. The Ursuline sisters nursed her back to health and also encouraged her return to the faith. Mary agreed and attended the High Mass the next day in celebration of coming to church again. She wore a beautiful blue dress and a white veil fashioned for her by the nuns for the special occasion.

In 1903 Mother Amadeus left Montana for Alaska to continue her missionary work. She bid a fond farewell to her dear friend Mary Fields, who was not only too advanced in age to accompany her, but too old even to continue the arduous mail route. Thus Stagecoach Mary, around seventy years old, retired at last from that job and moved permanently to Cascade. She began to settle into town life, where she opened a laundry service in her home. By then everyone had seen through Mary Fields's rough exterior, and people rushed to patronize her business. The generosity she'd shown in connection with her failed restaurants was well known; now people stepped up to assist her. R. B. Glover, the owner of the Cascade Hotel, provided free meals for her. Even when he leased the hotel to Kirk Huntley in 1910, it was with the condition that the meals would still be provided to the aging Mary Fields. In 1912, when Mary was eighty, her home was ravaged by a fire. The townspeople donated their time and supplies to rebuild her home and laundry.

Mary seemed to mellow as the years went by. The townspeople entrusted the care of their children to her to babysit, and she showered her charges with treats. She spent hours in her beautiful garden, tending her many flowers. Catholic services were held at Wedsworth Hall, and Mary took pride in decorating the altar with the flowers she had cultivated. She became an avid fan of the town's baseball team and even became their mascot. Besides traveling with the players to games, she took care of their bats and saw that those who hit home runs were rewarded. Mary made bouquets for the big hitters on her team and gave flower boutonnieres to the players on both sides. But if an umpire dared to make a call against her team, Mary's temper would come into full force once again.

The old and young of Cascade came to love Mary Fields. She was a colorful character, and though she spent many an hour in the town's saloons, her honor was never questioned. Her quick wit, her eagerness to talk politics, and her caring ways endeared her to everyone. Legendary cowboy film star Gary Cooper clearly remembered seeing Mary Fields in Cascade when he was nine years old. She herself was just past eighty at the time, and he was most impressed by her great bearing, her capacity to put away liquor, her excellent marksmanship, and of course the wreaths of smoke emanating from her cigar.

Though Mary never knew the exact date of her birth, she celebrated her birthday twice a year. The schools either closed down for the celebration or dismissed early whenever she declared it was her birthday, and Mary would give candy to the children. The celebration of her eighty-third birthday was a town event—Mary had been around Cascade for some thirty years. Ribbon badges were distributed that read MARY FIELDS 1830–1913: BIRTHDAY ANNIVERSARY MARCH 15, and a good time was had by all.

Mary Fields, who took great pride in always holding her own, saw her health begin to decline in her remaining years. She reluctantly spent the last month of her life in bed. The fiercely independent soul tried to slip away without burdening anyone when death was imminent. Taking her blankets with her on a cold December night, she lay down in a field outside her home to await death. As fate would have it, Lester W. Munroe and his three brothers came across Mary in some tall weeds; she was very near death. Their parents, Mr. and Mrs. D. W. Munroe (the second mayor of Cascade), were summoned, and Mary was brought to the Columbus Hospital in Great Falls. Every comfort was given to her. There she died from a severe case of dropsy (edema).

Her death on December 5, 1914, was marked by the entire town as the passing of a legend. The townspeople made sure every detail of her funeral was seen to. The service was held in the Pastime Theatre and was one of the largest in Cascade history. The abundance of floral arrangements was seen as a tribute to the townsfolk's beloved neighbor, and many friends came to pay their last respects. A priest from St. Peter's Mission said her Mass; leaders of the town served as pallbearers. Mary Fields was laid to rest at the foot of the mountains in the Hillside Cemetery that led to St. Peter's Mission.

Today the ruins of this mission are all that remain, but the legend of Mary Fields lives on. Her home was moved from its original site and became the living room section of the Herman Wolfe Ranch 1½ miles north of Cascade. Sixty years after meeting the legendary Mary Fields on the streets of Cascade, Gary Cooper stated that she was "one of the freest souls ever to draw a breath or a thirty-eight." And many early Montanans were the better for having known her.

At Long Last

Jane Manning James

J ANE ELIZABETH MANNING LOOKED DOWN at the trail of bloody footprints in the frost-covered ground. She was leading her family on a pilgrimage to Nauvoo, Illinois, in the fall of 1843. The weather had taken a turn for the worse, and the Mannings' feet were bare from their 800-mile cross-country trek. Jane would later recall, "We walked until our shoes were worn out, and our feet became sore and cracked open." It was a sacrifice these Mormon converts were willing to make.

Jane Manning was living in a small hamlet on the Norwalk River called Wilton, Connecticut, when she had first learned of the Mormon Church, which was founded in 1830. When she heard missionary Charles Wesley Wandell preach, Jane hung on his every word. She was convinced that he spoke the true gospel and that Joseph Smith, the leader of the Church of Latter-day Saints (LDS), was indeed a living prophet.

Within one week's time Jane Manning was baptized into the new faith. Three weeks later she claimed to have received the gift of tongues and to have had a vision in her dreams of the Prophet Joseph Smith. Jane's expression of faith convinced her relatives that the restored gospel of Jesus Christ was the truth, and they, too, converted. The Mannings planned to join their brothers and sisters in the Gospel, called saints, who were helping to establish God's kingdom on earth in Nauvoo.

Twenty-two-year-old Jane Manning had worked as a domestic for a wealthy farmer named Joseph Fitch since she was six years old, supporting her mother and four siblings after her father died. Her life was not an easy one, and before she was eighteen, Jane had also given birth to a son, Sylvester, on March 1, 1838, as a result of a relationship with a white minister—a man she trusted, but who took advantage of her. Her mother took in the baby because they needed Jane to continue working, but it may have been Sylvester's birth that started a longing in Jane to find a better spiritual home and a better life for her family.

Jane departed Wilton for Nauvoo and a new life in 1843 with hope in her heart. Her five-year-old son, Sylvester, her mother, two sisters, two brothers, a sister-in-law, and a brother-in-law joined Wandell's missionary party on the pilgrimage. Their plan was to go by boat along the Erie Canal to Buffalo, New York, and then on to the next stop in Columbus, Ohio. However, the Mannings did not have the money for the full fare, and no one in the Wandell party was either willing or able to pay for the Mannings' passage, so Jane and her family separated from the company and continued the 800-mile journey on foot. Before setting out, Jane arranged to have her trunk of belongings taken ahead on the boat.

Jane Manning had her faith tested on this long trek to Illinois. She and her family found what food they could to sustain themselves and braved the elements along the way. Their bloody footprints left imprints in the ground after their shoes were worn through. They prayed for assistance to complete their journey, and Jane recalled that they had "asked God the

Eternal Father to heal our feet and our prayers were answered and our feet were healed forthwith." Onward they marched.

In the mid-1800s traveling through new territory could be dangerous even for free blacks like the Mannings. Escaped slaves were often apprehended by the authorities at state borders and river crossings, and as blacks, the Mannings were assumed to be slaves until they could prove otherwise. In Peoria, Illinois, Jane and her family were held and interrogated as to their free status. This was confusing for the Mannings, who had never needed such documentation before— and they narrowly escaped jail.

Hardships were many. The Mannings waded out into freezing-cold water up to their necks to ford a river with no bridge. Jane had faith the Lord would see them through and counted her blessings. "We went on our way rejoicing, singing hymns, and thanking God for his infinite goodness and mercy to us, in blessing us," said Jane.

Upon arriving in Nauvoo, however, on a bend of the Mississippi River, they were not welcomed with open arms. Jane and her family certainly must have looked like a motley group, and they experienced "all kinds of hardship, trial, and rebuff." Then they met Brother Orson Spencer, who directed them to the "Nauvoo Mansion," home and headquarters of the Prophet Joseph Smith.

Joseph Smith's wife, Emma Smith, warmly greeted the Mannings, inviting them into her home: "Come in! Come in!" When Jane saw the charismatic 6-foot-tall, blue-eyed Smith, with his light-colored hair and skin, she immediately recognized him as the man from her vision.

Jane's remarkable story of leading a determined band of converts on foot impressed Joseph Smith. He asked her to recount their pilgrimage to guests gathered at the mansion, commending her for her undaunted faith. The Smiths took the Manning family into their home until homes and employment could be secured for them.

Within a week's time lodging and employment were found. Jane's five-year-old son, Sylvester, lived with Jane's mother. Her brother Isaac Manning became a cook at the mansion. Meanwhile Jane waited for the trunk that she had put aboard the boat at Buffalo, but it never arrived. She was despondent over the loss of her belongings, and because no position had been found for her yet. When Joseph Smith found her crying about her situation, he invited her to work as a servant in his household. Jane was thrilled with the opportunity. She took great pride in presenting herself well and in serving the prophet's family. Jane identified more with the white members of her new religion than with members of her black race.

Jane's acknowledgment by the prophet and the kindness shown to her by the Smiths furthered her religious fervor. She felt especially close to Joseph Smith, who greeted her warmly every morning and shook her hand. Jane was becoming more accepted into the Mormon inner circle. She was pronounced a true believer for her acceptance of the fact that Joseph had multiple wives, part of Mormon doctrine at the time. She was once given the privilege of holding the sacred stones that had been wrapped up in his garments. (The stones of Urim and Thumim aided Joseph Smith in translating the Book of Mormon, one of the four standard works of authorized scripture.)

Emma Smith offered to adopt Jane into her family as a child of God. Jane felt honored, but unfortunately did not understand the implication of the proposition. She turned down a second offer several weeks later. This decision would come to be the biggest mistake that Jane would ever make—one she regretted to her dying day. By being adopted into the Smith family, she would have received a temple "sealing," which would have united her in an eternal family relationship.

Jane longed to be accepted in the Mormon Church when she arrived in Nauvoo, Illinois, in 1843. Unfortunately though, the church's antislavery stance wavered under pressure, which affected her being welcomed with open arms. The church's first concern was its own acceptance in society. Proslavery non-Mormons in Missouri pressured the Mormons to leave the state. When Joseph Smith ran on a third-party ticket for the U.S. presidency in 1844, he openly opposed slavery, advocating that slaveholders be compensated for freeing their slaves. Ultimately, the controversy over the slavery issue and public opinion caused Joseph Smith to close the Nauvoo mansion as tensions between Mormons and non-Mormons increased. This left Jane without work. While she and her sister went to Burlington, Illinois, to secure jobs, disaster struck.

Anti-Mormon sentiments had escalated to the point that Joseph Smith and his brother Hyrum were arrested during a protest for inciting a riot. On June 27, 1844, a mob rushed the jail in Carthage, Illinois, where the pair were being held, and the Mormon prophet and his brother were murdered. Jane Manning was devastated by the news. "When he was killed, I liked to a died myself," Jane said.

Understandably, tensions simmered between Mormons and non-Mormons in Illinois after the murders. Jane went to live with and work for the new president and leader of the church, Prophet Brigham Young. During this time she married a free black man named Isaac James, also a convert. Isaac and Jane James were not to stay long in Nauvoo, though. Brigham Young directed the Mormons to abandon the town and move farther west to escape persecution.

Brigham Young found such a place in the desolate Salt Lake Valley located in Utah Territory. His master plan was to organize a mass exodus of all his people. Jane and her husband and her son, Sylvester, aged eight, decided to follow Brigham Young. Jane had remained true to the Mormon religion, but her extended family had lost faith after the murder of Prophet Joseph Smith and chose not go west with her.

En route to the Salt Lake Valley, Jane and Isaac James's first son, Silas, was born to them in Keg Creek, Iowa. They then continued on to Winter Quarters, near present-day Omaha, Nebraska. Winter Quarters provided a temporary place of rest and consolidation for the transient Mormon flock during the winters of 1846 and 1847. Of the thousands who wintered there, more than 300 died from inadequate food and shelter.

In June of 1847 Jane and her husband and two sons left Winter Quarters and continued on to Utah. They were in the lead company following in the footsteps of Brigham Young, who had left two months earlier with an advance group. The Mormon companies were well organized, with each group of one hundred being divided into more manageable subgroups, but still the journey to Utah proved very difficult. They forded rivers, encountered all sorts of inclement weather, and did not have adequate food or forage for their animals. The final 100 miles before reaching the valley were the most difficult of all.

Jane's company of ten was sent ahead for reinforcements, arriving in the Salt Lake Valley in September 1847.

In the Salt Lake Valley, the Mormons looked out for one another. All the pioneers had to overcome many hardships in the early years. The Jameses were the first free black family to settle in Utah, and although Jane had a minority status in her community, she earned the respect of the Mormon majority. Jane gave birth to a daughter in 1848. She strove to lead an exemplary life and became known for her generosity. She reached out to fellow saints through her continual acts of caring. In 1849 Jane shared two pounds of flour—half her own total—with her neighbor and friend, Sister Eliza Partridge Lyman, who had nothing to feed her family. Jane recalled the torment of hearing "my little ones crying for bread, and I had none to give them, but in all the Lord was with us and gave us grace and faith to stand it all."

In time the Jameses' financial resources improved through hard work. They purchased a home and farmed the land. Jane did the best she could for her son Sylvester. He had made her proud when he joined the Nauvoo Legion, which was the Mormon militia. He guarded their people and was prepared for combat with neighboring Indians when land disputes arose. Just as things seemed easier for the Mormon transplants, a plague of crickets and grasshoppers came and destroyed the crops in the valley. But the community persevered.

By 1860 Jane had six more children. They lived together in Salt Lake City's First Ward (one of the geographically defined areas that designated congregations), where they'd become the fifth-most-prosperous family. But then in 1869 Jane and her husband, Isaac, divorced after twenty-five years of marriage. He left her with all the children to support, the youngest just ten years old. Isaac sold his share of their holdings to Jane for $500. With her financial stability gone, Jane spun cloth, sold her homemade soap, raised food in her garden, and took in laundry to make ends meet. She moved her family to the Eighth Ward, where she lived out her life in a two-story house with a white picket fence.

In spite of her lowered circumstances, Jane's generosity continued and extended beyond her own ward. She was actively involved with the church's Relief Society, a women's auxiliary that provided basics for the needy. Most women donated homemade or homegrown items, but Jane donated cash from her laundry services at a time when currency was scarce. She was sometimes the recipient of the Relief Society's Christmas food baskets, yet she still made contributions. Jane also donated to the building funds for several temples over the years.

Jane Manning James was a pillar of strength through all the trials she endured. Between 1871 and 1874 three of her children died. Two daughters, Mary Ann and Miriam, died in childbirth at ages twenty-two and twenty-four. And her son Silas died of consumption at age twenty-five. Jane bore these heartaches and praised the Lord for her blessings. She did all she could to help her family, including giving part of her homesite to another daughter and taking in her grandchildren.

Four years after her divorce from Isaac James, Jane married Franklin Perkins. Jane's son Sylvester had married Franklin's daughter Mary Ann. Jane's second marriage was dissolved after just two years. Though life on earth was not easy for Jane, she focused on spiritual matters.

As Jane Manning James had understood the Mormon religion, the church professed equality before God for all people, regardless of skin color. In 1830 the Book of Mormon, considered holy scripture, stated that the Lord "denieth none that come unto him, black and white, bond and free, male and female." Therefore Jane felt that she should enjoy the privilege of full fellowship within the LDS Church. However, after her conversion to Mormonism, she came to understand that she was indeed considered inferior because of her race. Jane began to deeply regret not accepting Emma Smith's offer of being adopted into Joseph Smith's family in 1843 after first meeting the prophet and his wife. In 1849 Brigham Young had banned black males from the priesthood, and the tide of acceptance for blacks changed. In fact slavery existed in Utah from 1852 to 1862.

Jane remained faithful to the Mormon religion despite the church's vacillating views over blacks both in church and in society over the years. Mirroring the prejudices of the time, the Church of Latter-day Saints placed restrictions on the membership of blacks as it sought to find an acceptable place for them.

Nearing the end of her life, these restrictions caused Jane to become increasingly concerned about the afterlife because according to her faith certain temple ordinances that were not available to her as a black woman were necessary for salvation. In 1884, when she was around sixty-four, she began contacting church authorities to make specific requests to receive those ordinances. She had been a church member for forty-two years.

She dictated a letter to Prophet John Taylor, who was church president. Her request was to receive her "endowments," or special blessings given to worthy members in a solemn temple ceremony. She asked to be adopted to Joseph and Emma Smith's family as their child—reminding him that the offer had been made years ago, before she realized its meaning. This "sealing" would ensure a union beyond the grave, uniting them for all eternity. Jane also wanted these blessings for her ancestors and requested that the endowments and sealings be performed for them vicariously so that they would all be connected as one eternal family.

In 1888 Jane's request for adoption was denied, although she was granted a recommendation to enter the temple and baptize and confirm her dead relatives. She was told to be satisfied with being able to do this "work for the dead"; she should wait upon the Lord for further instructions. Her request for endowment was refused.

In 1889 Jane's first husband, Isaac James, returned. He wished to reestablish his relationship with Jane and the church. Jane forgave him and cared for him until his death two years later, even holding his funeral service at her house.

In 1890 Jane again contacted the church leaders to request adoption, reminding them of the previous offer and her connection in living with and working for Prophet Joseph Smith. Jane Manning James worked every angle she could to be granted the privilege of receiving her endowments so that she could achieve exaltation, the highest level of the celestial kingdom. She asked to be sealed to a deceased black man, Walker Lewis, who had been admitted to the priesthood before the ban was put in place. This sealing, she thought, would help her attain her endowments. She also asked to receive endowments for all her deceased relatives now that she had been extended the privilege of baptizing her dead.

By 1893 only eight of her eighteen grandchildren were still alive. In 1894 her son Jessie had died at age thirty-seven; in 1897 another daughter died, also at thirty-seven. The great sorrow in her life was that she outlived all but two of her children who had reached maturity. Jane had a strong sense of family and a strong faith. It is no surprise that she wished her relationships with her loved ones to extend beyond the grave.

Despite all her worldly setbacks and reverses, Jane's focus remained on the spiritual world. In 1893 she dictated her autobiography to be read at her funeral. In it she recounted her life story, enumerating her trials and her good deeds—conveniently not mentioning anything that might not put her in a good light, such as having a child out of wedlock and two failed marriages. Most assuredly she was hoping that at her funeral one day the church authorities would see the error of their ways and grant her the endowments she so coveted.

In 1894 she requested a personal meeting with the church president to ask for her endowments. He agreed that she was a longtime member of the church and a faithful one at that but told her that his hands were tied. Church officials found justification in biblical doctrine that denied blacks full inclusion in their faith.

The Latter-day Saints follow the King James version of the Bible. They believe the Bible to be the word of God as far as it is translated correctly, which for them is a literal interpretation. When Cain killed his brother Abel, he was cursed by God and "marked" for his sin. The Mormons made the assumption that the "mark" was dark skin and believed that blacks were descended from Cain. Additionally, Noah's son Ham married a descendant of Cain. A child from that marriage, Canaan, was cursed by Noah and doomed to servility. In Mormon scripture, a "blackness came upon all the children of Canaan, that they were despised among all people." These beliefs allowed the Mormons to insist on the inferiority of the black race—their lineage was tied to Cain.

Until the church president, or living prophet, received a revelation reversing that thinking, Jane would have to wait for her race to be redeemed. One year later Jane appealed her case. Once again her request to be sealed to Prophet Joseph Smith's family was denied, as were her endowments. However, it was conceded that she could be adopted into Smith's family as a servant.

In 1897 Jane and her son Sylvester partook in celebrating the fifty-year anniversary of the Mormons' arrival in the Salt Lake Valley. Jane had been a member of the LDS Church for fifty-five years. She had begun asking to be granted temple ordinances in 1884 and had continued to do so with great dignity over the intervening years. The church did grant Jane a privilege in recognition of her service to the LDS Church. She and her widowed brother Isaac Manning, who had come to Utah forty-five years later and reactivated his LDS membership, were given reserved seats in the front center of the Salt Lake Tabernacle when services were held there twice a year for General Conference and other important meetings.

The leaders of the church continually denied her requests for temple ordinances, but Jane never found their answers to be definitive. When church officials died and new prophets assumed leadership, she was hopeful the new prophet would have a revelation. She came back time and again to see if the position had changed.

In 1903 Jane dictated a letter to Church President Joseph
F. Smith, nephew of the martyred church founder, to see if it
was possible to receive her endowments. It was not to be. She
never received full inclusion into the faith to which she'd
devoted her life. Jane had wished that the church authorities
could see into her soul, but the color of her skin prevented
them from doing so. She had tried to change their minds for
twenty-four years.

Jane Manning James went to her grave with her requests
unfulfilled. She died on April 16, 1908, at almost ninety years
of age—she had continued to work to support herself and her
family until just a few years before her death. Her funeral
service at the Eighth Ward meetinghouse was well attended;
several church officials spoke. Jane was commended as a
faithful member of the LDS Church for sixty-six years.

For Jane Manning James, hope was the glimmer of light in
the dark tunnel of discrimination. She died with the hope that
in the future, it would be revealed that blacks could receive the
blessings and be entitled to full salvation. Church President
Joseph F. Smith spoke at her funeral and stated that one day
Jane Manning James "would in the resurrection attain the
longings of her soul."

Seventy-five years after her death, Church President
Spencer W. Kimball received a revelation that lifted the ban on
black male priesthood and allowed for all blacks to be full
members of the Church of Latter-day Saints. In 1979 Jane Elizabeth Manning James finally received her endowments.

Two years later a monument to Jane Manning James was
dedicated in the Salt Lake Cemetery next to her headstone. A
bronze relief on a granite stone shows Jane offering two

pounds of her meager flour rations to Sister Eliza Lyman, reminding us of the worthy life she led. Elder David B. Haight, descendant of Isaac Haight, captain of the first ten on Jane's journey to the Salt Lake Valley in 1847, spoke of Jane's loving nature at the dedication ceremony. At long last Jane Elizabeth Manning James had earned her just reward and was fully accepted into the church she was devoted to.

THE COMPLETE INSTRUCTOR

Abby Fisher

NEAR-PERFECT WEATHER ADORNED THE BEAU-tiful City by the Bay during San Francisco's great social event of the season. It was late summer 1880, and throngs of residents and visitors mingled about at the fifteenth Mechanics' Institute Fair. It was the place to see and be seen.

Crowds of people from every walk of life gathered in the vicinity of the Mechanics' Institute Fair pavilion. The massive two-story wooden clapboard building was erected on the east side of Eighth Street, extending between Market and Mission Streets. It housed thousands of exhibits to which curious spectators flocked. Outside, a band could be heard in the background and voices called out to one another in greeting, all laid over the multitudes of conversations and rumblings that contributed to the din of the fair.

The Mechanics' Institute had been established in 1855 as a way to help California's gold-rush economy transition to an industrial and agricultural one. The institute aimed to offer technical and mechanical arts classes to produce skilled workers for the growth of the industry, build a library, and gather the latest in scientific apparati. The fair was a popular outgrowth of these goals. Their intent was to promote local industry with exhibitions of new technology, manufactured products, and agricultural goods. It was truly a place to see the latest and greatest.

People would sometimes come several times a week during the fair's exhibitions, bringing money to finance the institute. There was almost too much to take in, from the art gallery, to the exhibits of machinery, to the floral displays—not to mention the elaborate 6-foot-high soap archway advertisement for the Standard Soap Company, the latest invention in the printing industry, the photographic studio, the afternoon and evening concerts, or the illuminated prismatic fountain at the north end.

Horse-drawn carriages pulled up under the overhanging veranda unloading passengers. Ladies in their fancy dresses and matching parasols were escorted by gentlemen in their finest attire, showcasing the latest fashions. They strolled gaily about the mechanics' and manufacturers' fair, mixing in with politicians, businessmen, vendors, common folks, and noisy children. For four glorious weeks—from August 10 to September 11— upward of 600,000 people would walk underneath the WELCOME banner that gently flapped in the wind atop the fair's entrance.

To forty-eight-year-old Mrs. Abby Fisher, entering as both an exhibitor and a contestant meant money in the bank. Abby Fisher was known a fine cook, and she was confident that the best of her pickles, sauces, jellies, and preserves would earn her a medal. As Abby Fisher walked around her booth admiring the fruits of her labor, she thought about how far she had come.

Abby Fisher had lived in the Deep South for the better part of her life. Like her mother, she was born in South Carolina and had been a slave. According to census records she was a mulatto—of mixed black and white parentage. Her father was a white man from France; presumably he was the owner of the plantation where Abby was born.

It is surmised that Abby was a favored slave on the plantation she grew up on, perhaps because of being fathered by her master. She never worked as a field hand. Instead she had worked in the plantation kitchen, learning to cook from the women before her. At some point Abby moved to Mobile, Alabama. In 1859, when she was twenty-eight, she married Alexander Cotchet Fisher, a mulatto man two years her junior. Another indication that she was shown special consideration was that her family unit had remained intact. Abby stated that she had "given birth to eleven children and raised them all." Typically slave children were sold off by their masters; that her family remained together may have indicated privilege.

Abby Fisher learned to cook traditional southern fare such as fricasseed chicken, corned-beef hash, and southern stuffed ham. But her southern African American dishes such as sweet potato pie, breakfast corn bread, and okra gumbo simply could not be outdone. Southern cuisine was greatly affected by African influence. Some of the ingredients that had made their way across the Atlantic from Africa were eggplant, watermelon, rice, okra, sorghum, and black-eyed peas. When slaves were allowed to grow their favorite foods in their gardens, they eventually made their way to the tables of the plantation owners for whom they cooked. Africans introduced their fruits, vegetables, and spices, combining them with foods found on the new continent such as sweet potatoes, corn, and pumpkin. Black women in the kitchen, like Abby, blended two cultures, and their knowledge and use of spices and herbs added a distinctive flavor to the foods. Abby Fisher was a master at combining the ways of her people with southern foods to create unique tastes.

Mrs. Fisher and her family continued to live in Mobile, Alabama, until 1877 when they moved to California. There were thirteen mouths to feed, and perhaps Abby and Alexander Fisher were enticed to take their family west to California by tales of greater economic opportunity. There are no records relating just how the family got to California, but most likely it was over the Oregon Trail, which left from Missouri where their daughter Millie was born. Wagon trains heading over the Oregon Trail were always in need of cooks, so it's possible that Abby offered her services in return for passage west.

Upon her timely arrival in California, the very resourceful Mrs. Fisher capitalized on her talents as a cook to support her family. San Francisco's wealth was beginning to transform the city from the rough-and-rowdy frontier days of the 1850s to a more refined and cultured city. The social character and makeup of San Francisco were unique. California gold and railways had created sudden prosperity. Wealth could propel a person into the upper echelon of society practically overnight. It wasn't just the lavishly decorated, spacious mansions or dress that indicated affluence; it was how you entertained—grand dinner parties were expected. Mrs. Fisher and her services as a cook and caterer for wealthy San Franciscans were soon in high demand.

Most of Abby's patrons were leaders and preeminent men and women in San Francisco. William Glascock, a lawyer from Virginia, and his wife, Margaret, who was from North Carolina, were wealthy clients who resided in Oakland. Edwin M. Miles, a stockbroker from Maryland, and his wife, Mollie, from South Carolina, lived in San Francisco. Her clients included the Harrolds, who owned Empire Extract of Malt, and William Gould, who was an actuary for the Pacific Mutual Life Insurance Company; his wife represented the Women's Franchise League at the 1893 Congress of Women in Chicago. Abby's reputation drew the attention of those who espoused excellence in dining. It was an impressive accomplishment for a former slave.

In addition to the catering, Abby Fisher and her husband started their own business in the production of pickles, preserves, sauces, brandies, and fruits. The 1880 U.S. Census listed Abby's husband as a "Pickle and Preserve Manufacturer" and her as a "Cook." However, the San Francisco city directories listed their business as "Mrs. Abby Fisher & Co." or "Mrs. Abby Fisher, Pickle Manufacturer." Clearly it was Abby Fisher's name, reputation, and culinary skills that were the driving force behind the success they achieved as partners.

Besides managing the catering and manufacturing businesses, Mrs. Fisher was busy raising her eleven children. By 1880 the older ones were most likely out of the house, either married or working. Their son Benjamin, then sixteen, was listed in the census as working as a messenger at a broker's office, perhaps for one of Abby's clients, either E. M. Miles or Charles S. Neale, both of whom were stockbrokers. Eliza Jane and Jennie, aged twelve and ten, were listed as students. Millie was just three years old.

As word of Mrs. Fisher's culinary skills got around, she found herself presenting her pickles, sauces, preserves, and jellies at the San Francisco Mechanics' Institute Fair in 1880. Abby had already been awarded a diploma—the top award—for her entries the year before at the 1879 Sacramento State Fair. She must have been confident that she would do as well at the new venue in San Francisco.

There were forty-five categories of exhibitions at the fifteenth Mechanics' Institute Fair that could claim certificates of merit, diplomas, or awards. The fairs were well on their way to becoming annual events, and Abby was surely pleased to present her homemade delicacies to consumers. She entered preserved fruits and vegetables, blackberry brandies, pickles, homemade vinegar, sauces, jellies, and jams. It was a marketing paradise that assured her of pure unadulterated advertisement.

Food products came under Division 6. Mrs. Fisher's entries were entered in Class 33—"Groceries, Flour, Meats, etc." The judges, W. W. Dodge, Samuel Foster, and Jacob S. Taber, were to award twenty-four premiums: one diploma, fourteen silver medals, and nine bronze medals. Abby Fisher had the great distinction of being awarded two medals: a silver for her "Assortment of Jellies and Preserves" and a bronze for her "Pickles and Sauces." Each medal was encased in a box and presented with "an elegant premium certificate." Most certainly the prestigious awards helped her sales.

Though no prizes were awarded in 1881, Mrs. Fisher again entered her wares, no doubt to the delight of the fair's attendees. Her secret recipes were described as thus by the jurors in the Industrial Exhibition Report: "Her pickles and sauces have a piquancy and flavor seldom equaled, and, when once tasted, not soon forgotten."

Abby Fisher made up her mind to author a cookbook, having been implored to do so by her many patrons. They were afraid that otherwise her delicacies would be lost to future generations. In spite of the seemingly insurmountable obstacle in accomplishing this goal surely was the fact that Mrs. Fisher could not read and write.

San Francisco was becoming known as a publishing and printing hub, and the Women's Co-operative Printing Office,

PREFACE AND APOLOGY.

The publication of a book on my knowledge and experience of Southern Cooking, Pickle and Jelly Making, has been frequently asked of me by my lady friends and patrons in San Francisco and Oakland, and also by ladies of Sacramento during the State Fair in 1879. Not being able to read or write myself, and my husband also having been without the advantages of an education—upon whom would devolve the writing of the book at my dictation—caused me to doubt whether I would be able to present a work that would give perfect satisfaction. But, after due consideration, I concluded to bring forward a book of my knowledge—based on an experience of upwards of thirty-five years—in the art of cooking Soups, Gumbos, Terrapin Stews, Meat Stews, Baked and Roast Meats, Pastries, Pies and Biscuits, making Jellies, Pickles, Sauces, Ice-Creams and Jams, preserving Fruits, etc. The book will be found a complete instructor, so that a child can understand it and learn the art of cooking.

Respectfully,

MRS. ABBY FISHER,

Late of Mobile, Ala.

I take pleasure in referring, by permission, to the following of my friends, namely:

WM. F. BLOOD..................415 California Street, San Francisco
E. M. MILES ....413 Montgomery Street, San Francisco
WM. O. GOULD..................512 California Street, San Francisco
MRS. CHARLES S. NEALE ....1814 Sutter Street, San Francisco
MRS. JOHN HARROLD..............416 Chestnut Street, San Francisco
MRS. W. H. GLASCOCK........... ... .Oakland
MRS. G. H. COY .. .. .431 Geary Street, San Francisco
MRS. JOHN C. FALLS. .... San Francisco
MRS. LOUIS H. VANSCHAICK....... .....129 Page Street, San Francisco

---

owned by the very confident Mrs. Agnes B. Peterson, became Abby's publisher. The firm was ahead of its time in employing female typesetters and was especially concerned with women's employment rights. Most likely the office would have been very sympathetic to assisting a female in getting her cookbook published recognizing, of course, the need to transcribe Mrs. Fisher's work in order to preserve some of the best southern cooking of their day.

Abby Fisher compiled all the recipes in her head and dictated them, creating the first published cookbook by a former slave woman. This regional cookbook—*What Mrs. Fisher Knows About Old Southern Cooking, Soups, Pickles, Preserves, Etc.*—was published in 1881.

Mrs. Fisher proudly claimed that her thirty-five years of experience in the "art of Cooking" qualified her to publish her often requested recipes. She wrote, "The book will be found a complete instructor, so that a child can understand it and learn the art of cooking." The lack of details in some recipes suggests that an experienced cook would be able to fill in the gaps, such as bake in a "quick oven" or add a "gill (½ cup) of milk." Her directives such as "never stir rice while boiling" and to boil corn on the cob for exactly seven minutes as "a longer cooking than this will take all the sweetness from the corn" are valuable tips.

What Mrs. Fisher Knows included 160 recipes in its seventy-two pages, divided into thirteen categories, from sweets to meats, and croquettes to soups. Her pickles, sauces, and preserves are full of southern flavor. Some recipes are not for the fainthearted, such as Ox-Tail and Calf's Head. She worried that a dictated version of her recipes might not "give perfect satisfaction." Her Circuit Hash is most likely a recipe for succotash; Jumberlie is certainly a drier version of a recipe for jambalaya; and Carolas are crullers.

There are no records that would imply how Abby Fisher was affected by her success with her businesses and cookbook. But surely her life was changed for the better, for there is evidence that she made personal improvements. In 1859, when Abby and Alexander Fisher were twenty-seven and twenty-five respectively, and presumably had been freed, they were able to have their marriage sanctioned by law. By that time they had had seven of their eleven children. The 1900 U.S. Census listed her at age sixty-eight and her husband as sixty-six; both were able to read and write. By then they may have sold or closed their business as "Pickle and Preserve Manufacturers": Alexander Fisher's occupation was listed as a janitor, and no occupation was given for Abby. By 1900 they had been "married" for forty-one years and owned their own home at 440 Twenty-Seventh Street free of mortgage. Their home was west of San Francisco Bay and sat in the very scenic foothills near Mounts Davidson and Sutro. Two daughters, Jennie and Millie, aged thirty and twenty-two, remained at home with them. What is most surprising is that they no longer listed their race as mulatto, but rather as white. Being racially considered black all her life, she may have been light enough to pass as white, and certainly more doors were open to whites.

What Mrs. Fisher Knows About Old Southern Cooking, Soups, Pickles, Preserves, Etc. seemed all but forgotten for nearly a century. Then it came to the public's attention when the rare cookbook was put up for auction at Sotheby's in 1984. The Arthur and Elizabeth Schlesinger Library on the History of Women in America at the Radcliffe Institute for Advanced Study now owns the cookbook.

In 1995 Applewood Books, a publishing house that seeks primary-source materials, reprinted *What Mrs. Fisher Knows*—114 years after its original publication. It is a thin paperback reproduction, with the addition of notes by a culinary historian. After sitting neglected for more than a century, this truly African-southern cookbook is now recognized as a culinary treasure rich in historical value.

Mrs. Fisher's cookbook provides insight into what life was like in days gone by. Her vast knowledge of herbal medicinal recipes tells about what illnesses people suffered. With her *Blackberry Syrup – For Dysentery in children* recipe she claims, "This is an old Southern plantation remedy among colored people." The statement to slice cucumbers "the thickness of a silver half-dollar" tells about the currency of the day. Thus a cultural account of daily life is given in the regional preferences of certain foods she used.

Today Mrs. Fisher is appreciated for the great contributions she made to our nation's culinary history. She is recognized at the Henry Ford Museum/Greenfield Village in Dearborn, Michigan, one of America's greatest history attractions and the largest indoor-outdoor museum. Twelve indoor acres house treasures and artifacts from the past, while eighty outdoor acres hold historic homes and structures. There amid the Wright Brothers' workshop, Rosa Parks's bus, the Susquehanna Plantation, and an authentic Model T automobile is "Mrs. Fisher's Southern Cooking" seasonal lunch stand. Constructed near the Ackley Covered Bridge, the stand offers cuisine taken from her cookbook, including jumberlie, chicken gumbo, circuit hash, corn bread, chicken salad, and sweet potato pie, not to mention fried chicken, fried catfish, and hush puppies. Even Mrs. Fisher's famous coconut pie is offered in a cafe, though the recipe has been modernized. (The coconut is no longer placed "in a hot oven and let it stay long enough for the shell to pull off.") The cookbook is available for purchase for those who long to replicate some fine southern fare. It is a rare and delightful read.

Abby Fisher spent her whole life practicing and perfecting her craft. She clearly had come to the right city to succeed as a cook, a caterer, a manufacturer of fine prepared foods, and an author when she arrived in San Francisco. Her journey from the plantation slave kitchen to successful entrepreneur and published author is an amazing one.

UNBROKEN BOND

Clara Brown

CLARA BROWN BURIED THE TEAR-STREAKED face of her youngest child in the folds of her calico dress. Her world was being turned upside down, and there was nothing Clara could do about it.

The marketplace was bustling with activity on that sweltering Kentucky day in the mid-1830s. In the center of the square, amid the commotion of vendors hocking their wares and farmers selling their produce, was the slave-auction block upon which stood families who were being torn asunder.

Thirty-six-year-old Clara Brown witnessed her family being divided up like pieces of property with price tags on their heads. She watched in abject horror as Eliza Jane was wrestled from her arms. The terrified ten-year-old girl, recently traumatized by the drowning of her twin sister two years earlier, was lifted onto the block. The child's trembling knees could barely support her frail frame. There she stood before the crowd, defenseless against the world as potential buyers sized her up. Words could not explain the anguish Clara felt, but she dared not utter a word of protest for fear of making things worse for her daughter.

In what seemed like slow motion to Clara, little Eliza Jane was whisked away in the back of a farmer's cart along with some feed, lumber, and bolts of fabric. The frightened look in Eliza

Jane's eyes imploring her mother to save her would haunt Clara all her years. Clara resolved at that moment that she would track down this precious child of hers if it took the rest of her life.

Clara took her turn on the auction block next. Devoid of any feeling, she stood in a trancelike state. She had vague memories of being sold along with her own mother when she was just three years old. But her clearest memory was when their master, Ambrose Smith, moved to Russellville in Logan County, Kentucky, in 1809. Clara had lived there ever since she was six years old. She had married at age eighteen, borne four children on the Smith farm, and mistakenly assumed she'd always live there. Had the tobacco farm continued to turn a modest profit, Clara's family would not have had to be sold. After Master Smith died, however, his family was forced to sell his property and slaves to settle the estate. Thus Clara's family was separated, and she was sold George Brown of Russellville, Kentucky.

Clara soon learned that relatively speaking, she was better off than many other slaves. Her new owner, Master George Brown, a hatter, was of the merchant class, not a farmer. Clara settled in her new life as a domestic in the Brown household. Compared with being a field hand, where labor was grueling and hours were long, this was an improvement. For twenty years Clara took care of the Browns' house, did the laundry, and helped raise the Browns' three daughters, Mary Prue, Lucinda, and Evaline. Even though she was loved and respected by the family, not a day went by without longing to be with her own loved ones. She could only hope that her family had fared as well as she had and trusted that the Lord would protect them.

Clara Brown
COURTESY DENVER PUBLIC LIBRARY,
WESTERN HISTORY DEPARTMENT, Z-275

Clara's determination to keep track of her family was aided by George Brown's kind inquiries, which kept her informed of their whereabouts over the years. Her eldest daughter, Margaret, had been sold to Mr. Bednigo Shelton near Morgantown, Kentucky. Clara remained in contact with her until Margaret died. Her son, Richard, grew to adulthood, but because he was sold so frequently she eventually lost track of him, as well as her own husband. Little Eliza Jane had been sold to James Covington of Logan County, Kentucky, but in 1852, when Eliza Jane was twenty-six, she was sold to a new owner, and Clara could not locate her again.

When George Brown died in 1856, Clara's life again changed dramatically. Master Brown's last will and testament stated that Clara, one of his three slaves, was to be awarded her freedom along with $300. For legal reasons that remain unclear, Clara Brown technically had to be put up for auction before gaining her freedom. The Brown daughters, who had a special affinity for Clara, arranged to purchase her, agreeing to pay three-quarters of the price that she went for if Clara would pay the other part to gain her freedom. Surely it was a most confusing and frightening turn of events for Clara, as the bidding went to $475. Good to their word, the Browns paid the price. Thus at age fifty-three Clara earned her freedom and set out to find the daughter who had been stolen from her twenty years earlier.

Kentucky law stated that former slaves had up to one year to vacate the state once they were freed. Patrollers, or watchmen, roamed the streets asking to see their freedom papers and Clara most likely kept her parchment in a pouch on a string under her clothes, as many freed slaves did. Clara's search for her daughter in the surrounding area proved fruitless. If Eliza Jane had been freed, Clara thought that perhaps she might have left Kentucky. So Clara departed for St. Louis, Missouri, the third busiest U.S. port, which she thought might have employment opportunities. Her plan was to set up a laundry business and look for her daughter.

After her search in St. Louis, Clara headed for Leaven-worth, Kansas, which had a population of 10,000 in 1858. A year in Kansas brought no news of her daughter, though. In fact, the talk in Kansas was of heading farther west. Gold was said to have been discovered in Colorado, and settlers were heading to Pikes Peak in droves. Perhaps Eliza Jane had joined the throngs searching for a better life. Clara decided she would go west, set up her own laundry business, and save her money. She would use her earnings to continue her search.

No substantial gold had been discovered yet in Colorado by the spring of 1859, but the gold rush was in full force nonetheless. Rumors of gold were enough to spur the '59ers on. The panic of 1857 had left all too many people financially ruined. The allure of the shining metal was as bright as the future that many envisioned for themselves out West.

Clara sought out a reputable wagon master named Colonel Wadsworth, who had a party of sixty emigrants in his thirty-wagon caravan. Her persistence and determination persuaded the colonel that he needed her as a cook on his overland journey to Colorado. The combination of her height and dark complexion, along with her high cheekbones and steely black eyes—inherited from her Cherokee grandmother—gave Clara a distinctive countenance. She was very convincing. Wadsworth agreed to transport her washtubs, scrub boards, and bins in exchange for Clara cooking for a mess of twenty-five of his men. Thus at age fifty-six Clara found herself on a 700-mile trek across the country.

In mid-April 1859 the caravan left Kansas for Cherry Creek, Colorado (present-day Denver), but they were not alone. More than 100,000 settlers, prospectors, gamblers, outlaws, confidence men, and law-abiding citizens were also heading west in search of their fortune. They lumbered on for eight weeks across the plains as Clara cooked, cleaned, washed, and served the men. She prepared meals of buffalo and venison, beans, greasy bacon, biscuits, dried apples, and coffee.

It wasn't until May 6, 1859, that Colorado gold was revealed as a sure thing. Georgia prospector John Gregory discovered the famous Gregory Gulch Lode near Central City, Colorado. News of this spurred on those en route, but others did not believe it. By the end of the summer, some 50,000 settlers thought it a fool's dream and were returning home from the "Cherry Creek humbug." An endless parade of defeated Pikes Peakers streamed eastward early on, eager to sell their mining equipment and supplies to the westbound emigrants, who like Clara, remained hopeful.

On June 6, 1859, Clara's wagon train arrived in Cherry Creek, which comprised the rival twin cities of Denver and Auraria on opposite sides of the South Platte River. Denver's growth was slightly in the lead of Auraria's, with 150 shanties or tent houses established, but both communities were lawless, rough-and-ready places.

Clara had not come to pan gold herself, but to make money off those who did. By 1860 there were forty-eight freed African Americans in Colorado, only two of whom were laundry women. The scarcity of women to cook and launder for the miners meant that there was always available work. The towns were overflowing with desperate miners hoping not just to strike it rich, but to survive each day until they did.

Clara empathized with those who were struggling to make it, and her heart went out to those even less fortunate than her. She opened the doors of her humble abode to anyone in need of food and shelter, and before long she became known as Aunt Clara to everyone. She tried to help civilize the area, offering her cabin to host prayer meetings and assisting two Methodist minister friends when starting the Union Sunday School. Clara ended up staying in Denver for just six months, though. News of a mining town up in the mountains held the promise of a more lucrative laundry business, and she jumped at the opportunity.

Clara paid someone to take her meager belongings and the setups for her laundry business up the steep incline first to Gregory Point, at an elevation of 8,500 feet, then to Mountain City (later Central City). The "city" consisted of one perpendicular street alongside the Gregory Lode that intersected two parallel streets. Hadley Hall, which was a grocery and mining supply store on the first floor, had a performing stage/church hall on the second floor. Clinging to the side of the steep hill were the tents, shanties, and cabins that made up the mining camp.

There was plenty of money to be made as a laundress, and Clara was in great demand. She charged fifty cents to wash the miners' blue and red flannel shirts—the equivalent of two pinches of gold dust. Clara worked from her two-room cabin on Lawrence Street hauling water to boil for the washing, gathering wood, and chopping it to stoke the fires. She scrubbed the laundry on her washboard, wrung out the heavy clothes, and hung them up to dry before ironing them.

Clara accumulated great wealth through this backbreaking work over the years. It was a laborious job that she would hold well into her seventies. She wisely invested her money in real estate, partnered with several male friends and advisers in business transactions, and "grub-staked" with the growing community of miners whom she befriended. For this Clara would receive a portion of their claims when they proved up in return for food and laundry services. This turned out to be a substantial source of income for Clara. By the time the Civil War ended, she had accumulated more than $10,000. Through all this time she had entreated everyone she had met to inquire for her into the whereabouts of her daughter Eliza Jane. She truly believed that one day her prayers would be answered.

The miners' hard-earned money was often spent in the many saloons that lined the muddy alley called Main Street, where a pinch of gold dust bought a shot of whiskey. Clara knew that the way to uplift this mining-town home of hers was to bring some semblance of civilization. To her that was accomplished through charitable acts toward others, the influence of women and families, and the building of churches. Clara offered food, shelter, and nursing care to others regardless of race or ability to pay. She contributed generously to the Presbyterian Church, to which she belonged, as well as the Congregational Church. She was among the ten members who organized the St. James Methodist Church in Central City and had offered her home as a place of worship before they organized in 1860. There again she helped start a Sunday school.

In 1865, after slavery had been abolished, Clara felt it safer to travel throughout the country. That summer, at age sixty-two, she returned east, searching for her daughter and any family she could find. Clara offered a $1,000 reward for news of her daughter and had letters of inquiry sent all over the country. She searched in Logan County, Kentucky; in Sumner County, Tennessee; and across the surrounding areas, all to no avail. The emancipated slaves she encountered were destitute and homeless. Once again her heart opened wide. Clara returned home to Gilpin County, Colorado, with a family of sorts—almost thirty friends, acquaintances, and orphans who were searching for some family to belong to. She had arranged over-land transportation for the freed slaves.

Clara's acts of kindness and her desire to find her daughter seemed to have no bounds. In 1879 thousands of destitute African Americans from the Deep South had made a mass exodus to Kansas, where it was rumored there were job oppor-tunities. Kansas could not handle the glut of all these "Exo-dusters." At seventy-six Clara acted as an official representative of Colorado's Governor Pitkin, traveling by train to Kansas to intercede on their behalf. She brought word of financial sup-port and job opportunities available in Colorado's mining towns—all the while, of course, searching for Eliza Jane.

Eventually Clara's continual search for her daughter, her support of local churches, the money she sent to educate young women back east at Oberlin College as well as aiding those whom she brought to Colorado, and her many countless acts of charity dwindled her savings. She had suffered financial set-backs from people who took advantage of her trusting nature and from the fire loss of her home and properties. By her late seventies she was destitute.

But the people of Colorado—recognizing a lifetime of good works—came to Aunt Clara's aid. It was time for Clara to accept some of the kindness she had always shown others. After twenty years in Central City, she was convinced to leave the mountain town and move to the warmer climate down in Denver. A white frame home was provided for her at 607 Arapahoe Street, and a pension for old pioneers was given to her.

Incredibly, Clara Brown's prayers were finally answered in February 1882 when she was almost eighty years old. A letter arrived bearing the news that Eliza Jane had been located. A chance conversation between a woman who had once lived in Denver and a woman in Council Bluffs, Iowa, revealed that Eliza Jane Brewer and Clara Brown were indeed mother and daughter. Eliza Jane clearly remembered the traumatic details of her early life and that her mother had lived with the Browns in Russellville, Kentucky.

Clara Brown was nearly beside herself in finding her long-lost daughter. She was overcome with joy and shouts of praise for the Lord. A telegram was sent to Eliza Jane confirming the kinship. News of dear old Aunt Clara Brown's impending reunion was published in the newspapers, and aid rushed in. The half-fare train passage Clara already owned was turned into a full fare, and monies were provided for clothing and travel tickets to and from Iowa. Her friend and caretaker, A. G. Rhoads, provided food for the trip from his Rhoads' Steam Bakery (which later became part of the National Biscuit Company, known today as Nabisco). At long last the seventy-nine-year-old mother could hold her fifty-six-year-old daughter.

Clara Brown arrived on the Denver Short Line Train on a rainy day with a heart that was surely breaking with joy. The rain could not dampen the souls of the two women who were to be reunited after forty-seven years of separation. In the muddy streets of Council Bluffs, Clara exited the streetcar and looked toward the corner of Broadway and Eighth Street. There stood her little Eliza Jane, looking for her mother. An ecstatic mother and daughter ran through the mud, overcome with emotion. Clasped in each other's arms, with tears of joy streaming down their faces, they rocked each other and somehow ended up sitting in the mud, each refusing to let go of the other. A lifetime of prayers had been answered.

The women had decades to catch up on. Eliza Jane Brewer brought Clara's granddaughter Cindy with her back to Denver. Eliza Jane was a widow with nine children (her husband had died in the Civil War).

Eliza Jane came to know how much the residents of Colorado respected her mother for her years of charitable work. In the spring of 1884, prominent society ladies in Denver arranged a benefit on Clara's behalf. Her neighbor, Mrs. A. J. Jacobs (later known as a founder of United Way), invited the mayor, bankers, justices of the peace, and business leaders of Gilpin County to contribute a purse for "dear old auntie."

The Gilpin County Pioneers recognized Clara Brown as a notable pioneer renowned for the charity she had shown to early settlers in need. In 1884 the Colorado Pioneer Association accepted Clara Brown as its first woman member and provided a stipend. Eliza Jane accompanied a delighted Clara to the 1885 meeting where she was honored.

Clara Brown died of a heart ailment on October 26, 1885, with her beloved Eliza Jane, her granddaughter Cindy, and many others who considered themselves her family and friends at her side. Clara would have been amazed at the ways people found to honor her. The Colorado Pioneer Association took care of all her funeral arrangements. The ecumenical service at Central Presbyterian Church in Denver would have pleased Clara, with all her church affiliations. The funeral procession at Denver's Riverside Cemetery was replete with those whose lives she had touched. Crowds of people attended her service: Miners, prominent society people, business leaders, politicians, military men, ministers, the old and the young, and people of all colors came to pay their respects.

Today Clara Brown's memory lives on. In Denver's state capitol a stained-glass image of her hangs in the Old Supreme Court Chamber. The Central City Opera House dedicated a chair in Clara's honor in the 1930s. A plaque at the Saint James Methodist Church in Central City notes that services were once held at Aunt Clara Brown's home. She was inducted into the Colorado Woman's Hall of Fame. In 2003 an opera, *Gabriel's Daughter,* was written chronicling her life. Additionally, students of African American heritage attending any Colorado university can apply for a paid internship program dedicated to her memory. All this to honor a woman who showered others with acts of kindness after love was taken from her.

Clara Brown's abiding faith in the good Lord permeated every aspect of her life. Her remarkable ability to forgive was exemplified when she was asked if she held any resentment or bitterness toward those who had shown injustice to her during her lifetime. She replied: "Lord bless you, no, dey has suffered enough."

HOME SWEET HOME

Annie Box Neal

ANNIE RAN TO THE CORNER OF CONGRESS
and Warner as fast as her little feet could carry her. She burst
through the door of the *Tucson News Depot* clutching two sheets of
crumpled paper in her hand. She stood there moving her hand in
syncopated rhythm with the musical notes she had scrawled upon
the papers, totally absorbed in her own world. Ten-year-old Annie
Box had come for her piano lesson. It was clear to her instructor
when Annie began to play her composition that "Oklahoma
March" was something special. The piece was rife with passion.

Young Anna Magdalena Box understood hardship and sorrow
well. She had been born on a cold January evening on a Cherokee
reservation in Oklahoma in 1870. Annie's mother, Hannah Box,
who was just sixteen at the time, was part Cherokee Indian and part
black. Her father, Wiley Box, was of black and white parentage.
Growing up, Annie had often heard tales of her grandmother's grueling 1,000-mile journey to Indian Territory; she had been among
those forced to walk over the Trail of Tears in accordance with the
U.S. government's Indian Removal Act.

Annie too had experienced a long march of her own. When
she was around six years old, her family decided to leave the reservation, joining a small caravan of hopefuls headed for the Arizona
Territory. The trip proved to be an arduous one for Annie. Leaving
the flat plains of Oklahoma, they traversed the mountainous terrain

of New Mexico and then the valleys and canyons of Arizona. The weather ranged from blazing heat to bitter cold; from parching winds to pouring rain. Their wagon rolled on through barren plains to sandy desert stretches, then steep rocky hills. Food and water were often limited, and renegade Indians were a real threat.

Annie's parents, Hannah and Wiley Box, resorted to a variety of jobs to make a living after leaving the Oklahoma Territory. Her father's preferred trade was gambling, so they went from one frontier town to another in search of gambling opportunities and invested their winnings in mining claims.

Sometime between 1876 and 1879, the Box family reached Tucson. Work was hard to come by in that pioneer town in the late 1870s, which made for a transient lifestyle. Annie's parents decided to enroll her in a boarding school to provide her with some sense of stability as well as an education. When she was nine years old they dropped her off at St. Joseph's Academy, "So the sisters can learn her something." Located in the heart of Tucson on Broadway Street, the academy was directly attached to San Augustine's Mission. The Catholic nuns educated Annie and the other miners' daughters.

Though book learning in general was not Annie's forte, she was passionate about her other interests such as painting, cooking, and especially music at which she excelled. She became Sister Cabello's shadow in the kitchen, drinking up every bit of knowledge she could about cooking with the fresh fruits and vegetables from the convent's beautiful gardens. Annie was unaware that the skills she was gaining would set her up for life.

Unfortunately Annie's education lasted only until she was fourteen. She left St. Joseph's Academy to join her parents prospecting

Annie Box Neal
COURTESY ARIZONA HISTORICAL SOCIETY, TUCSON, AH-22073

in the hills of the surrounding mining towns until they settled down and purchased a house on Convent Street in Tucson.

Annie grew up into a beautiful, confident, and flirtatious young woman who had apparently inherited the best characteristics of each of her parents. Her skin was caramel colored and her black hair was tightly curled. She was light of foot and very tall, with a soft voice that did not match her 6-foot frame. Stunning and full of life, Annie had no lack of suitors. By seventeen she had been married twice, though both marriages failed.

Annie Box finally met her match in William "Curly" Neal. Curly was a friend of the Box family whom Annie had met when she was sixteen. He was twenty-one years her senior and had been married once before. The two seemed to have a lot in common. He too, had been born in the Oklahoma Territory and had lived on an Indian reservation as a child. Like Annie's mother, he was part Cherokee and part black. Annie was high spirited and was drawn to his wild side; Curly had served as a scout for Buffalo Bill Cody for four years in the army.

Over the next seven years, Curly had endeared himself to the Box family, including Annie and her younger sister Josie. Curly was headstrong, honest, and well liked. A dignified and refined Annie was more social than he. The two got along well, but could both hold their end in an argument. Annie and Curly fell in love. On January 4, 1892, twenty-two-year-old Annie Box married forty-three-year-old Curly Neal in San Augustine Cathedral in Tucson next to the mission boarding school she had attended as a child. Satisfying her passion for music that she had fostered at school was yet to come.

The couple lived in Oracle, Arizona, a mining town in the Santa Catalina Mountains. It had been founded in 1880 and still wasn't much of a town more than a decade later. But Annie would change that. Her husband was busy managing a stage route that was the only transportation between Tucson and the surrounding towns. While he transported supplies, passengers, and the U.S. mail, Annie took an interest in accompanying him on the days he moved gold bullion. The delivery of this bullion to the Consolidated Bank in Tucson provided plenty of adventure for Annie. Often she rode shotgun with Curly on his stage runs from the Mammoth Mine to the bank in town. She loved the thrill of sitting atop the stagecoach with her gun, no doubt feeling bulletproof. She was ever ready to prevent would-be bandits from stealing the gold ingots. Annie was a natural with a gun, and her sharpshooting skills were superior; she was not one to be easy on the trigger.

Annie's life took a terrible turn when she lost her dear mother, Hannah, on April 9, 1894. It was an incalculable loss for the twenty-four-year-old. She and Curly adopted Annie's six-year-old sister, Josie, but even taking part in the girl's upbringing did not console Annie. She withdrew more and more from life. Nothing her husband could do would bring her out of her grief. At long last Curly thought of a grand plan to bring his Annie back. The gift he'd give her would be a project that would occupy her time, capitalize on her talents, and bring music back into her life.

Curly's stage line hauled freight and passengers within a 100-mile radius of Tucson. Day in and day out, he brought passengers along the relatively level but dusty few hours' ride to the Acadia Ranch, a hotel that doubled as the first health institution in Oracle. E. S. and Lillian Dodge ran the ranch as a hotel and sanatorium for tuberculosis victims. The Acadia had received national attention and acclaim from the *Journal of the American Medical Association,* which highly recommended the resort's climate.

The town of Oracle was known for its natural beauty. It was 40 miles northeast of Tucson, seemingly in the middle of nowhere, but the climate was unsurpassed. At 4,500 feet above sea level, the pleasant weather was suitable for both health and recreation. It provided the perfect getaway during the hot summer season, which lasted for seven months. And mild temperatures during the winter months were conducive to comfortable breathing for those stricken with pulmonary afflictions. With doctors sending patients out West for the clear, dry, dust-free air, a health resort seemed sure to see big profits.

While the Acadia Ranch did have a general store and a post office, it was no more than a ranch house with a number of cottages and two large wells. The guests who frequented the ranch were distinguished, wealthy, health-seeking people who were willing to travel long distances for their well-being and pleasure. That gave Curly the idea of offering a resort on a much grander scale—and he knew that his Annie could manage such an enterprise perfectly.

Over the years the combination of the Neals' land acquisitions, mining claims, their large 3N Ranch (named for the three Neals: Annie, Curly, and Josie), and their other successful business ventures provided them with great wealth. Additionally, their property in the heart of Oracle was perfectly situated amid the scrub oak trees in the foothills of the 9,000-foot-high Santa Catalinas.

Perhaps Annie gradually began to look at their 160-acre property—with its spectacular mountain views, lush green grass, and oak-shaded lawns—in a new light. She grew intrigued by the idea of a grand resort hotel, but wanted to take it a step further. Besides a plush resort, it would also be a recreational playground for the very wealthy. People could seek out their hotel not just to recuperate, but for pleasure as well. Annie decided to take on the project and would see that their hotel offered only the finest amenities. As proprietor she would be in charge of the design, the furnishings, the management, and all the activities the hotel would offer.

The opulent Mountain View Hotel was to be situated on the Neals' land, half a mile from their 3N Ranch among its corrals, stables, and bunkhouses. Construction was begun in June 1894. Nine months and $90,000 later, it was completed.

Annie proved relentless in overseeing the building of the structure and the ordering of the furniture and decor. The 50-by-46-foot brick hotel sported two stories with 2-foot-thick adobe walls. The exterior had a stucco coating painted to resemble red brick. Vines and mulberry trees added to the ambience. Each level had extra-wide central halls that extended the length of the hotel. The great halls measured 14 by 40 feet and were used as gathering rooms. On the perimeter were six spacious, lavishly decorated guest rooms. Both floors featured spectacular verandas that encircled the building to take in the beautiful mountain views. The upper rooms had stoves; the lower, fireplaces. One indoor bathroom with hot and cold water was located on each floor. The main building was connected by a covered porch to a two-story structure measuring 21 by 48 feet. Its first floor housed the kitchen and dining area. On the second floor was the spacious multipurpose recreation room.

Annie's attention to detail was impeccable. Expert craftsmen were hired to outfit the oak-and-walnut interior. Patterned tin ceilings hung over the lofty, exquisitely decorated rooms. Miraculously, Annie had everything in order on time to open for business. The *Arizona Daily Citizen* ran an article a month prior to the opening titled "A Charming Resort: . . . Tucson's Favorite Mountain Resort and Health Sanitarium . . . Unexcelled for Summer and Winter Residences." Invitations for the gala affair were extended to notable guests, prominent and distinguished citizens, and all who wanted to see and be seen.

The editor of *Arizona Star* covered the grand opening of the Mountain View Hotel on February 19, 1895. It was a spectacular event. Festivities and music lasted into the early-morning hours, and the attendees agreed that it was a night that would be long remembered. People marveled at the elegant decor and beautiful square area rugs that brightened the rooms. Wine and champagne from the wine cellar flowed freely. The food was fit for a king, with a menu featuring fresh fruit and vegetables from the hotel's lavish gardens. Every imaginable delicacy had been prepared; even the garnishes were works of art.

Favorable accounts of the Mountain View Hotel were featured in newspapers and magazines around the country, bringing phenomenal success to Annie's grand establishment. Before long it was being touted as "Tucson's Favorite Mountain Resort and Health Sanitarium." For $10 to $12 per week, guests could experience what was once described as the "Epitome of Western opulence." Financiers, authors, health and pleasure seekers, and wealthy bachelors and debutantes looking for a suitable mate—all found their way to Annie's hotel. People came from the East Coast, the West Coast, everywhere in between, and even from around the world. Annie had a flair for the art of entertainment with musical accompaniment and was renowned for her gracious hostessing. She was kind, caring, and genuine. Such treatment attracted the wealthy, who relished being pampered. Annie Neal thought of every comfort and anticipated her guests' every need.

The Mountain View always featured an interesting mix of people, from celebrities to local ranch hands. Annie designed the billiard room on the second floor of the smaller building to serve as a meeting hall, hold church services, or be transformed into a dance floor. There was also an outdoor pavilion twinkling with colored lights for dancing under the stars. Annie's music was always a part of the Mountain View Hotel. The orchestra's melodious tunes wafted out through the windows into the cool evening breeze. The parlor was filled with a piano and various instruments for those who were musically inclined. Perhaps her own "Oklahoma March" punctuated the air with its crisp notes. There was a nine-hole "golf course" of sorts. Carriages of all types, bicycles, horses, and burros were available for rental.

Annie provided medical staff for those who had come to recuperate from illness by breathing in the clean, clear mountain air. All dietary needs were met with delicacies fresh from the gardens. The windmill brought up ice-cold well water purified by running through granite. Annie even provided teachers so that guests' children would not fall behind in their studies.

Perhaps Annie's greatest talent was as activities director. She orchestrated dances, put together picnics, and established hiking outings. She brought together guests of the nearby Acadia Ranch and her grand Mountain View resort for games of croquet, card tournaments, and whist competitions. Annie even set up "race days"—actually rodeos. Great outdoor feasts and celebrations followed the races. There were shooting matches with team mascots and statisticians to record both the men's and women's scores. The *Arizona Daily Citizen* and the *Arizona Daily Star* eagerly carried results of the amiable, but serious sporting events between the two resorts, held for the prize of a traveling trophy in the form of an olla, a wide-mouthed earthen water vessel. Today the Acadia Ranch Museum in Oracle, Arizona, houses the olla trophy.

Distinguished guests, well-known in their day as well as multi-millionaires, and prominent local families all frequented the hotels, hailing from nearly every state as well as countries as far away as China, Russia, and Australia. The register from the Mountain View Hotel is now housed in the Arizona Historical Society Library in Tucson. It lists the names of the movers and shakers in society and foreign nobility. Treasure hunters came in search of the Lost Escalante Mine somewhere in the Santa Catalina Mountains. Annie heard the stories from her husband, Curly, who believed that the mine was real. She even hosted Harold Bell Wright at the Mountain View while he wrote *The Mine with the Iron Door*, which popularized the legend of the buried gold. Hollywood turned the book into a movie about Oracle's lost mine.

Perhaps the most famous guest at the Neals' Mountain View Hotel was their good friend Buffalo Bill Cody, who came to check his mining claims in the area. Curly had worked with Buffalo Bill when he was nineteen, well before he'd married Annie. Cody and his famous Wild West Show troupe stayed at the Mountain View Hotel frequently between 1909 and 1916; he was a favorite with the guests who participated in race days. Annie was said to boast that the only shooting match she ever lost was to Buffalo Bill. On one of his visits, Cody played the role of Santa Claus in a mining camp in Oracle. After distributing gifts to children from near and far, Buffalo Bill participated in the races and the trapshooting and target-shooting matches. It was a day Annie would never forget.

Sadly, as time went by, the elite clientele who came to Oracle turned their backs on Annie by not including her in local social gatherings. She was invited to fund-raisers and always contributed generously, but her name was not found on guest lists for private parties. Still, Annie always held her head high before those who cast her out. She was well received by the townspeople of Oracle and Tucson, who knew her to be a woman of high moral standards with a generous, loving heart. She was a charming, soft-spoken, refined gentlewoman who was loved by many. Annie also served as Oracle's midwife and was given permission by the Catholic Church to baptize children. Though she had no children of her own, she was godmother to many.

Annie Neal's Mountain View Hotel enjoyed a successful run until the post–World War I era, which saw changes in the ways people were able to spend their disposable income. Curly sold their 3N Ranch and moved with Annie into the Mountain View. Annie's marriage to Curly Neal lasted forty-seven years, ending when he died in a freak accident.

The flow of distinguished guests who had enjoyed their home away from home died off to a trickle over the years. Annie sold the Mountain View in 1936, but continued on as manager even though she had been in poor health for a decade. On May 12, 1950, Annie Box Neal died at age eighty. Tributes were written in numerous newspapers about the "State Pioneer" who had resided in Arizona for seventy years.

The grand Mountain View Hotel was sold three times over the years. It was lovingly restored, but seemed stripped of its glory without the beautiful verandas, the music, the happy guests, and sweet Annie Neal. The Neal era was a memorable one for many health and pleasure seekers. The land between the Oracle Inn and Oracle Hill was referred to as Neals' Pasture for years after Annie's death. For those who were a part of the Mountain View Hotel in its heyday, there was no comparable experience out West. Annie Neal had a flair for making their home away from home as sweet as the music that graced its halls.

Free at Last

Mary Jane Holmes
Shipley Drake

Sixteen-year-old Mary Jane Holmes awoke early that morning as happy as she had ever been in her life. Her prospective groom, Reuben Shipley, was coming to Mr. Ford's house to ask permission to marry her. She had already given her handsome suitor an affirmative response to his marriage proposal, and she was elated to think that soon she would quit the home that she had been tending for years to start one of her own.

Her elation, however, quickly turned to despair. Mary Jane had been peering out the window watching Rueben as he spoke with Nathaniel Ford, who had long been her master. When she saw Rueben's face fall, she sensed all was not well—and when Rueben walked away dejectedly, she knew it. Mary Jane ran down the stairs and out after him. She soon learned that once again she was to be a pawn in Mr. Ford's game, which seemed at every turn to define her life.

It wasn't the first time that Mary Jane Holmes must have felt that Nathaniel Ford had two sides to him. She'd found that out as a child, before her family ever moved to Oregon.

The Holmes family had belonged to one Major Whitman, a paymaster for the army in Howard County, Missouri, for twelve years. In 1841, the year Mary Jane was born, the situation changed for her and her parents, Robin and Polly Holmes, and her older sisters, Harriet and Celi Ann. Whitman was deeply in debt, and Nathaniel Ford, then sheriff of Howard County, had the Holmes family sold to satisfy Whitman's creditors. The confusion came the next morning when Mary Jane's father, Robin Holmes, went to secure a wagon from the merchant who'd purchased them in order to move his family and their belongings to their new home. The merchant's wife informed Robin that her husband was gone on a business concern and she knew nothing about the purchase of any slaves.

Robin Holmes reported this mix-up to Sheriff Ford. Ford then told Holmes that an arrangement had been made for Ford to keep Robin Holmes, his wife, and their three girls himself. Consequently, the Holmeses worked as slaves for Ford for three years, never really knowing if the transaction was legitimate or to whom they truly belonged under the law.

In 1844 many people were leaving for the Oregon Territory in an attempt to make better lives for themselves. Nathaniel Ford, too, opted to head west, leaving unsettled debts behind him. Ford told Mary Jane's father that he needed his help starting a farm out West. The family was promised its freedom once the farm was up and running if they went with him to Oregon.

Thus in 1844 Robin and Polly Holmes found themselves traveling seven months over the Oregon Trail with Mary Jane and her sisters, all under the age of seven. The wagon train of hopefuls, guided by the experienced mountaineer Moses "Black" Harris, was among the largest caravan ever. All that stood between Mary Jane's family and freedom was the seven-month journey over plains, deserts, and mountains—and time spent establishing Mr. Ford's farm.

Mary Jane Holmes Shipley Drake
COURTESY OREGON HISTORICAL SOCIETY

On December 7, 1844, they arrived in the Oregon Territory. Nathaniel Ford set out to locate his claims in the Rickreall Valley. The men built cabins, and Ford allotted plots of garden space to the Holmeses to grow their own vegetables for sale. The Holmes family worked hard getting Ford's farm in Polk County established. By then Mary Jane was almost nine years old and had done her fair share of work along with her parents and siblings. During this period there were both happy and sad times for her family. In 1845 Mary Jane's brother, James, was born; in 1847 another sister, Roxanna, joined the family. Her older sister Celi Ann had died a few years before that.

In 1849, after five years of backbreaking work, Robin Holmes went to Nathaniel Ford to secure their freedom. But the master had one last request—and he was not to be denied. Ford wanted Robin Holmes to accompany him and his son and some of the men from the valley to California on a gold-digging excursion.

Lacking any other option, Robin left his wife and children in Oregon and headed for the gold fields to serve in the capacity as a miner and camp cook. He took with him Ford's promise to release his family upon his return, along with the assurance that he could keep some of his findings. The children waited for their father for one year.

When Robin returned in March 1850, he had $900 worth of gold in his possession. He hoped to obtain his freedom having now fulfilled Ford's request to assist digging for gold in California. He went directly to see Ford, who had returned to Oregon earlier due to illness. Ford granted Robin and Polly their freedom along with their youngest son, Lon, who had been born during Robin's absence, hoping that would satisfy

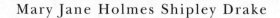

Robin Holmes and the local abolitionists who supported him. However, Ford intended to keep Harriet (thirteen), Mary Jane (nine), James (five), and Roxanna (three) until they all came of age—twenty-one for boys and eighteen for girls. He claimed that he had the right to do so since he had supported the children thus far and felt entitled to get more work out of them when they were older.

Ford was short on money. All his gold earnings, which he had put in his son's possession, were lost when his son died on his return trip to Oregon. Robin Holmes suspected that Nathaniel Ford's intention was to try to get him to pay for the rest of his children. Ford could demand a higher price for them based on their worth as slave property if they were adults.

Filled with anguish and lacking legal recourse, Robin Holmes took his diminished family and moved 5 miles away to the town of Nesmith's Mills, near Ellendale. There he had found employment at the mill and began to save his money. Ford had threatened to take the Holmes children back to Missouri where slavery was legal and sell them if the Holmeses attempted to get custody of their children.

When after two years nothing could persuade Nathaniel Ford to change his mind about freeing his other children, Robin Holmes took Nathaniel Ford to court. Robin and Polly Holmes had begun to wonder if he'd ever truly had legal possession of them at all, remembering the suspicious circumstances under which they'd come to be Ford's property back in Missouri.

Slavery had been declared illegal in the Oregon Territory by the Oregon Provisional Government in 1844, the year they had arrived. The ban on slavery and the enforcement of the exclusion laws were meant to prevent blacks from settling the area and were not necessarily reflections of Oregon's enlightened attitudes toward free blacks. The Holmeses knew that their chances of winning a case against a white man were slim, but it was the only way for the entire family to be reunited. Mary Jane's eldest sister, Harriet, had died during a visit to her parents in 1851. They blamed Ford for her death.

Robin Holmes felt that he would go forward with the lawsuit since some slaves had sued successfully for their freedom. He felt that he might succeed for the following reasons: His family may not have legally belonged to Ford in the first place; Ford had given Robin Holmes his word that he would free his family on several occasions; and slavery was not even legal in Oregon.

In 1852 Robin Holmes used his savings to engage the legal counsel of S. B. Wood and take Nathaniel Ford to court. Robin was uneducated, illiterate, and poor, but he was determined. Since Harriet had died, it was just Mary Jane, James, and Roxanna who were being held in slavery by Ford. Nathaniel Ford was well aware of the fact that those settlers who had brought slaves into Oregon after 1844 were supposed to give them up after three years, but he disregarded the ruling.

The legal battle to determine the Holmes children's custody was long and drawn out. It began on April 16, 1852, with the District Court of the United States of America in Polk County in the territory of Oregon. Sheriff W. S. Gilliam served a writ of habeas corpus to Nathaniel Ford, directing him to produce the allegedly unlawfully held minor children of Robin and Polly Holmes on the first day of the next term.

Nathaniel Ford responded on April 5, 1853, that he did indeed have said children in his care—but as his "wards," not his slaves, as per agreement with Robin Holmes. Ford further stated that the Holmeses were unfit parents because they were poor and uneducated. Robin Holmes insisted that the children were being held against their will in a territory that prohibited slavery; that he and his wife, Polly, were caring parents; and that Ford had reneged on his promises of freedom.

In the interim Mary Jane stayed in either the Ford household or in his married daughter's home as a servant. There she was able to witness the lengths to which Ford went to win. Nathaniel Ford had often threatened to take them all back to Missouri, where slavery was allowed, and sell them. Though Robin Holmes had no proof of such arrangements, he was further convinced of it by Ford's many delay tactics during the trial.

On April 16, 1853, Ford asked to delay the proceedings until he could produce a witness privy to a conversation held between Ford and Holmes in which the arrangement to keep the Holmes children had been made. Associate Justice of the Supreme Court of the Oregon Territory Cyrus Olney declared that the hearing be postponed until the next term of the Supreme Court in Salem. Ford put up the huge bond of $3,000 against the possibility of him leaving town with the children. All Mary Jane Holmes knew was that nearly a year had passed and she did not seem any closer to freedom.

For political reasons judges in the Oregon Territory were reluctant to address controversial slavery issues. Judge Olney thus temporarily split the custody of the children until the final hearing in an attempt to make some headway. Ford was awarded custody of Roxanna, and James was awarded to his parents. Twelve-year-old Mary Jane was left to make the difficult decision of where she wished to temporarily reside. Though she surely wished to return to her parents that would mean leaving five-year-old Roxanna alone at the Ford house. Mary Jane chose to stay. Her parents were allowed visitation rights. Both Ford and Holmes were to put up a $1,000 bond and promise to produce their respective children at the next hearing.

Robin Holmes finally asked the court to place Mary Jane and Roxanna in charge of the sheriff, as both he and his wife had previously been prevented by Ford from seeing their children. Though Nathaniel Ford claimed that he always treated his servants in a kindly way, Robin was fearful that the children might be being mistreated. He was still worried that Ford might attempt to sell them, where they would be lost to their parents forever. Robin made an "X" mark to serve as his signature on the application for a writ of habeas corpus on June 9, 1853, ordering Ford to submit the illegally detained children. Mary Jane and Roxanna were consequently placed in the custody of Sheriff B. F. Nichols by Judge Cyrus Olney.

Time came for the testimony of Ford's witness, General Joseph Lane, on July 5, 1853. General Lane remembered being at Nathaniel Ford's home in March 1850, but could only vaguely recall the conversation between Ford and Holmes. He said it "left an impression on my mind" that Holmes was to be freed, and his children were to stay with Ford, but he could not definitively say so. The man's testimony was worthless. Meanwhile the girls waited to be reunited with their parents and brother.

On July 13, 1853, the case was heard in Dallas Polk County. Judge George Williams, chief justice of the Territorial Supreme Court, had recently arrived in Oregon. He was eager to clear his docket and was willing to deal with the slavery issue head-on. *Holmes v. Ford* was moved to the top of his list. The judge made

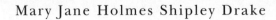

his decision based on the fact that slavery was illegal in Oregon. His final ruling stated:

> Said Judge having heard the allegations and evidence of the petitioner and Respondent orders and decrees that the said children Jenny, or Mary Jane, James and Roxanna be and they are hereby awarded to the care and custody of their parents Robin Holmes and his wife to be and remain with them as their children as fully in all respects as though they the said children had not been in the custody of the said Ford, and it is ordered and adjudged that the said Ford pay the costs of these proceedings and execution therefore.

Robin Holmes had come very close to losing his children forever. Ford had indeed tried surreptitiously to sell the Holmes family during the legal proceedings. A letter dated June 22, 1852, was obtained some time during the trial and was filed with the court offering proof that Mr. Ford had written to an attorney named James A. Shirley of Howard, Missouri. In the letter Ford poured out his soul, relating all his woes. He told of his family back home who would not answer any of his letters, of his daughter-in-law who'd died, of how he had become ill on his gold-finding mission to California, of how his son—who had been transporting their combined gold, worth $16,000, back to Oregon—had been either killed or drowned. He had a family of daughters to support, he continued, and was very poor except for 640 acres of land. He related that the Negroes he'd brought west had become a curse to him ever since abolitionists had put thoughts of freedom into their heads. He urged James A. Shirley to assist him by sending an agent West under the Fugitive Slave Law to apprehend Mary Jane, James, and Roxanna, as well as their parents and young Lon, who were already free, and take them back to Missouri to be sold. He was willing to pay all expenses. He went on to ask that the papers be left blank in order for him to put in someone's else's name, as he did not want anyone from Missouri to come after him for his old debts. Ford suggested a profit could be realized from the sale and "if the case of the Negroes can be attended to it will releave me and my fambly of much trouble and you may be benefitted." Ford had concluded his letter by asking that the deal be completed before the next setting of the district court. After discovery Nathaniel Ford claimed he had written the letter because he was tired of being harassed by Robin Holmes, not because he was trying to obtain any money for himself.

During the fifteen-month court proceedings, Mary Jane's parents had moved to Salem, Oregon. There they were involved in setting up a nursery business and most likely also sold produce from their garden. Settlers arriving in the area after their long trek over the Oregon Trail were always grateful for fruits and vegetables. Roxanna and James Holmes moved to Salem to live with their parents.

Oddly enough, Mary Jane Holmes continued to stay with the Ford family. No longer legally restrained or under the control of her former master, she was perfectly free to choose where she wanted to live. Perhaps she was paid for her services and wished to add to her family's income. Or she may have felt a loyalty toward the family she had worked for and lived with. It is thought that she worked for Ford's married daughter, Josephine Ford Boyle, helping her with the children in addition to helping Mrs. Nathaniel Ford. This arrangement with the Ford family lasted for four years.

Then in 1857, when Mary Jane was sixteen years old, she met her prospective groom, Reuben Shipley. Reuben was fifty

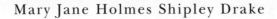

and had been married once before and had a family in Missouri, but the difference in their ages and circumstances did not bother Mary Jane. Back in Missouri, Reuben had been an overseer on a plantation separate from that of his wife and sons. He had come to Oregon in 1853, nine years after Mary Jane's own family had arrived, as his master also promised Reuben his freedom if he'd assist him on the journey to Oregon. So Reuben left his family behind, planning to save to purchase their freedom. He later learned that his wife had died; when he inquired about purchasing his sons, he was told that they would not be sold for any price. Mary Jane's heart went out to Reuben; the hardship and heartache she had experienced in her own short life allowed her empathy for his plight. She must have hoped that they would never have to endure a similar separation. She was eager to start a new life with him and start a family of their own.

Nathaniel Ford told Reuben Shipley that he would grant him permission to marry Mary Jane on one condition: Reuben had to pay $750 for Mary Jane's release. This made no sense to Reuben, Mary Jane, or her family, because she had been liberated by court order four years earlier. Mary Jane felt that she had done right by Mr. Ford in working for him and his family as both a slave and a servant. Perhaps it was while Mary Jane watched from her window and witnessed the conversation between Reuben Shipley and Nathaniel Ford turn sour that she finally decided that she didn't owe him her life.

The couple could have taken Ford to court, as he had no legal right to hold Mary Jane. Reuben Shipley was a well-respected man in his community and had many distinguished antislavery friends. Eldridge Hartless, for whom Reuben had worked after gaining his freedom, and the Reverend J. T. Connors, both white men, did not want to see him turn over any money to Ford. They urged him to fight. Mary Jane, however, knew all too well how long a court battle could be drawn out, and she did not want to undergo that again. Reuben Shipley had already lost one wife and did not want to be deprived of another. He paid the ransom rather than go through the court battle. Mary Jane and Reuben Shipley were married in 1857, free at last from any hold Nathaniel Ford held over her.

Mr. and Mrs. Reuben Shipley moved to a home near Mary's Peak in Benton County, 4 miles west of Corvallis, Oregon. Generally blacks in rural communities faced less prejudice than those in urban areas, and the Shipleys were not only socially accepted but were highly respected members of their community. They made a living on an eighty-acre farm that Reuben had purchased, where he planted oak trees for shade. Mary Jane and Reuben had six children together, three boys and three girls: Thomas, Wallace, Ella, Martha, Nettie, and Edward. The Shipleys were guests of distinguished Benton County white families, and their children played freely together as well. In 1861 Reuben and Mary Jane donated two acres of their land up on a hill to the county for the Mount Union Cemetery.

Throughout her life Mary Jane was active at the United Brethren Church in Benton County, and later in the African Methodist Episcopal Church. She certainly knew her share of sadness in life. She had seen the deaths of her three sisters; then in 1864 her youngest brother, Lon, was wrongfully accused of theft and nearly hanged. He died from injuries suffered during the ordeal. Sometime between 1867 and 1870, Mary Jane's mother, Polly, was committed to an insane asylum.

Nevertheless Mary Jane and Reuben created a comfortable life for themselves. They managed to acquire $2,000 in real estate and $865 in personal property, according to the 1870 census. Reuben died in 1873 at the age of sixty-six. Mary Jane stayed on their farm rearing their children, the youngest of whom had been born the year her husband died.

In 1875, when Mary Jane was thirty-four, she married R. G. Drake and continued to live in Corvallis until his death a few years later. They had no children together. In 1880 Mary Jane left her farm and moved to Salem with her two youngest children. Mary Jane is thought to have gone back to Corvallis during a typhoid epidemic; she is remembered by some in the community for assisting those stricken with the disease.

Mary Jane Holmes Shipley Drake moved to Portland in 1889 when she was forty-eight years old. She lived there with her only remaining son, Edward, aged sixteen, who worked for the Southern Pacific Railroad. She had outlived the rest of her children, one of whom died from smallpox. Though it is not known how the rest died, none of them lived past the age of thirty. Her youngest son, Edward, took loving care of her for years until she had a stroke and suffered some paralysis. Mary Jane then lived out her life at the Charlotte Homes for the aged at 472 Sellwood Avenue in Portland, visited often by her son. When she died in 1925, she was taken back to her home in Corvallis and buried in the land she had donated for the Mount Union Cemetery beside her husbands and children.

Newspaper articles claim that at her death, Mary Jane Holmes Shipley Drake was 101 years old. However, the court records from *Holmes v. Ford* indicated that Mary Jane was born in 1841, making her around eighty-four at the time of her death.

Contemporary articles also state that she was married to a Reuben Ficklin, not a Reuben Shipley; the discrepancy could be due to the fact that freed slaves sometimes took on surnames other than those given them by their former masters.

Mary Jane Holmes Shipley Drake never did take on the name of her master, Nathaniel Ford, but the lives of her family members were interwoven with those of the Fords. No ill will between the two families seemed to exist outside the custody issue. Remarkably, the relationship appears to have remained cordial.

In 1953, one hundred years after the court case, Ford's descendants attempted to clarify Nathaniel Ford's intentions. They insisted that Robin Holmes had begged Nathaniel Ford to take his family to Oregon with him, not that Ford took them as his slaves. Ford's descendants also stated that Ford did not ask for money from Reuben Shipley in order to marry Mary Jane Holmes insisting that: "Nathaniel Ford had no contact . . . with Mary Jane or her husband before or after they were married."

What is certain is that Mary Jane Holmes's life would never be her own until Nathaniel Ford released his hold on her. Fortunately Reuben Shipley realized that and claimed his bride.

The Second Act
Mary Ellen Pleasant

MARY ELLEN PLEASANT WAS A TALL, slender, young black woman with dark eyes and sharp distinctive features. The light-skinned thirty-five-year-old woman had no trouble finding work as a domestic in the homes of wealthy San Franciscans in 1849. Her employers were pleased by her stately bearing, her maturity, and the fact that she knew her place. They hardly took notice of her, but she certainly gleaned all she could from them.

While her employers and their dinner guests entertained themselves with talk of business, investment, and speculation, she pretended to busy herself with serving them their multicourse meals. Without anyone knowing her true identity or intentions, Mary Ellen Pleasant was privy to inside information of business transactions and lucrative deals—all of which she turned into sizable profits. Her performance was masterful.

Mary Ellen Pleasant's past is clouded by mystery, and her life itself is an enigma. Virtually every facet of her life is debated by historians—from her birthplace and parentage to her free status and her net worth. Some say that Mary Ellen was born a slave in Georgia, but she claimed she was born free in Philadelphia, at 9 Barley Street, on August 19, 1814. She believed that her father was a native Kanaka, from Polynesia, but it is rumored that he was a southern slaveholder or a Cherokee Indian. Her mother, a black woman, was probably from Louisiana.

What is known is that she was not raised by her birth parents. It was not atypical for children to be sent away if their parents had the opportunity to advance their offspring's station in life. When she was six years old, Mary Ellen was sent to live with a Quaker family, the Husseys, on the island of Nantucket, 30 miles off the Atlantic Coast. She stated, "I never knew why I was sent there, and about all I know is that my first recollections of life dated from Nantucket." The nature of her status with her foster family is uncertain. They were to see that she was educated, but instead they reportedly kept the money sent to provide that education for themselves. Whatever the case, Mary Ellen regretted the fact that she never received a formal education while in Nantucket. However, the lack of such did not keep her from becoming successful.

The facts of Mary Ellen's life are confusing, and perhaps she wanted it that way. She may have refuted rumors of a slave past hoping to distance herself from it. A connection to slavery may have been detrimental to a person's reputation or advancement in society. Or perhaps she had simply denied being a slave for so long that it became the truth for her.

While fact and fiction may never all be sorted out, Mary Ellen did leave Nantucket Island. When she was fourteen or fifteen, she returned to Philadelphia. She had grown into an attractive young woman who was very sure of herself. She became acquainted with a rather well-to-do black man, a Bostonian named James Henry Smith, who was an ardent abolitionist. The two fell in love and were married around 1833, when she was nineteen years old. Smith had a successful contracting business, and he and Mary Ellen used their money to support the Underground Railroad assisting fugitive slaves in Philadelphia. When

Mary Ellen Pleasant
COURTESY SAN FRANCISCO HISTORY CENTER, SAN FRANCISCO PUBLIC LIBRARY,
AAD-2997, FROM THE HELEN HOLDREDGE COLLECTION

her husband died after four years of marriage, he left Mary Ellen with two things: a sizable inheritance and his wishes for her involvement in the abolitionist movement to continue.

Mary Ellen moved back to Nantucket where in 1847, at age thirty-three, she married John James Pleasants, reportedly a former slave of John Hampden Pleasants, a second cousin of Thomas Jefferson. Her husband had lived in Virginia and New Bedford, Massachusetts, a hotbed of abolitionist activity. Moving back to the mainland, she became even more impassioned in her fight against slavery, and when a contingent of East Coast abolitionists moved to the western United States, she and her husband followed suit. Mary Ellen arrived by ship in San Francisco around 1849 (some accounts say 1852) during the gold-rush era. Her husband either came with her or arrived at a later date. They left behind her young daughter, Lizzie J. Smith, in the care of someone else.

Mary Ellen planned to capitalize on the opportunities that abounded in gold country. Whether it was by design or not, she realized that she could learn a great deal from the dinner conversations of successful businessmen whom she served. Their discussions offered plenty of opportunities to witness all sorts of business transactions and hear invaluable information. Mary Ellen needed to learn how to invest her fortune and these gentlemen knew a lot about making money.

Mary Ellen Pleasant (the *s* was later dropped from their name) once described herself in these words: "I am a whole theatre to myself." Indeed, it was quite an act she put on in San Francisco, one that involved masking who she really was and what she did. When she arrived in the city, good cooks were scarce, and Mary Ellen reportedly had people bidding for her services for up to $500 per month. No one suspected that their housekeeper, or mammy (as she was sometimes referred to), enjoyed a sizable inheritance. Researchers have speculated that she had from $15,000 to upward of $50,000 to her name.

Mary Ellen lent money to others at 10 percent interest and speculated in real estate and other entrepreneurial efforts. By 1855 she had purchased several laundries and small businesses. Her investments in property and the stock markets were sound, and she amassed great sums of money. She also spent a great deal of her earnings on worthy causes, befriended many in need, and took on protégés to promote their careers.

While Mary Ellen worked as a domestic, her husband, John Pleasant, was a cook on a sea vessel. They may not have always lived together, but for twenty years they worked in unison against the injustices of slavery. Little is known of their daughter, Lizzie. She did come west to California and was married to a Mr. R. Berry Phillips in 1865. Mary Ellen threw them a wonderful celebration, but Lizzie reportedly passed away while she was still in her twenties.

All the while Mary Ellen Pleasant worked, she never lost sight of her abolitionist leanings and continued to support many fugitive slaves. She even rode into rural areas challenging people who held slaves illegally. She paid to bring blacks west and found them lodging and employment when they arrived. Some say that she placed former slaves as servants in wealthy homes to glean investment information. Mary Ellen donated large sums of money to the Convention of Colored Citizens of the State of California. In 1858 she hid the fugitive Archie Lee in her home after his controversial trial. She and many black San Franciscans supported his right, and the subsequent right of all blacks, to live in the state unencumbered by others.

In 1859, when she was forty-five, Mary Ellen went to extreme measures in her passion to fight slavery. She traveled to Boston to learn more of John Brown's proposed slave insurrection. Brown, a militant abolitionist from the East, planned to raid the national armory and arsenal at Harpers Ferry, West Virginia. He was to use the stolen guns to organize a rebellion and establish a base in the Blue Ridge Mountains from which to rescue slaves. Mary Ellen Pleasant traveled to Chatham, Canada, where Brown resided, and funded his cause, contributing $30,000. Brown was to postpone the attack until Pleasant could arouse support by riding through the countryside disguised as a jockey alerting fellow blacks to the insurrection. Brown did not wait, the attack on the federal government failed miserably, and he was executed. An incriminating letter written by M. E. Pleasant was discovered on Brown's person stating: "The ax is laid at the root of the tree. When the first blow is struck, there will be more money to help." Fortunately the initials *M. E. P.* were misread as *W. E. P.* Mary waited for things to quiet down and then sailed back to California undetected under an assumed name.

Mary Ellen Pleasant fervently fought racial discrimination in San Francisco. In 1863 she was involved in the fight for black people's right to testify in a court of law. Then, on September 27, 1866, Mary Ellen was refused a ride on a San Francisco streetcar because of the color of her skin. She and her husband were involved in a two-year lawsuit against the North Beach and Mission Railroad Company (NBMRR), which resulted in her being awarded $500. In an appeal, however, the Supreme Court reversed this decision, stating that the NBMRR had not instructed the driver to refuse her passage; nor was it done with malicious intent. Because "no indignity, no oppression, no outraged or wounded feelings, no injured sensibilities appear in the case," Mrs. Pleasant was simply refunded her five-cent fare. Still, this case thrust her into the public spotlight as a crusader for civil rights. It wasn't until 1893 that an antidiscrimination law was passed.

In the late 1860s, when Mary Ellen Pleasant was in her mid-fifties, she devised another money-making scheme. She moved to San Francisco's Portsmouth Square and set up a boardinghouse that catered to the city's elite business and political circles, casting herself in the socially acceptable role of innkeeper. Once again nobody suspected otherwise. The financial wizards of her day made their way to her upscale establishment at 920 Washington Street, which provided a private arena for its high-class patrons to conduct business. Mary Ellen Pleasant made a point of getting to know anybody worth knowing in town and soon gained the confidence of such prominent men as David Terry, D. Q. Mills, W. C. Ralston, Newton Booth, and Lloyd Tevis. While she catered to and stroked the egos of investors, politicians, and well-connected businessmen, she took in every bit of inside information. As before, she used the profits she attained in precious metals, mines, stocks, and real estate to finance philanthropic activities and causes.

In 1877 Mary Ellen Pleasant built a sprawling thirty-room Victorian boardinghouse that covered two city blocks. The lavishly furnished $100,000 mansion on the corner of Octavia and Bush was dubbed the House of Mystery. Rumors as to exactly what went on inside the swank establishment were rampant. Its exclusivity made some raise their eyebrows; the place was often rumored to be a brothel. Indeed, Pleasant was the keeper of many secrets and very well could have provided such a service as a fringe benefit for her patrons, though there was never any proof of such. Others who wished to discredit Pleasant suggested that she worked voodoo on the men to keep them under her control. The accusations may have stemmed from people's inability to comprehend how a black woman could move so freely within white society.

Inside the mansion, on the other hand, Mary Ellen Pleasant was recognized as a shrewd businesswoman. Men were said to seek her out for exchanges of information. Since she knew and safeguarded their secrets, perhaps they in return honored the disguise she found it necessary to wear.

One such gentleman whom Mary Ellen came to know well was millionaire Thomas Bell, vice president of the Bank of California. He and Pleasant enjoyed a mutual admiration for each other's business acumen. They sought each other out for financial advice, and by the 1870s they had become business partners commingling their joint ventures. Bell was known as Pleasant's "personal friend and business partner," but when he took up residency in the mansion, the nature of their relationship came under suspicion. The rumors subsided when Thomas Bell married one of Mary Ellen's protégées, Theresa, but the suspicion never went away.

Some of the stances Mary Ellen Pleasant took and the causes she supported put her into the state and national limelight—and under the scrutinizing eye of a society not always eager to see her succeed. Pleasant financed the legal battle of another protégée, Sarah Althea Hill, in a highly publicized divorce from her very wealthy husband, the former U.S. Senator William Sharon from Nevada. The notorious case lasted four years, bringing Mary Ellen repeatedly to the witness stand. The defense lawyers and press had a field day trying to destroy her credibility—attacking her reputation, her business relationships, and her finances. They started rumors that Mary Ellen's mother had been a voodoo queen from Louisiana, and that Mary Ellen practiced voodoo herself. She survived the negative publicity of *Sharon v. Hill,* but not totally unscathed. The accusations against her character were damaging, and financial support for Sarah Althea Hill cost her $65,000.

Mary Ellen Pleasant sought refuge at her spacious ranch, Beltane, in Sonoma Valley, which she purchased in 1891. While it was a great getaway, her troubles continued to follow her. The next year, Thomas Bell died at Pleasant's Victorian Mystery House, and his death was ruled suspicious. Bell had fallen over a second-story banister to his death in the middle of the night. Once again the press tore apart Mary Ellen Pleasant, now seventy-three years old. It was rumored that she had pushed him over in an attempt to collect $100,000 from him. No evidence was ever presented, however; and when the will was probated, Pleasant wasn't even mentioned. The case was subsequently dropped.

For more than twenty years, the Bell family had lived in Pleasant's mansion on Octavia; Mary Ellen Pleasant had continued to manage all of their business and personal finances as well as social engagements. In 1897, five years after Bell's death, his eldest son, then twenty-two, challenged the legal guardianship of his own mother, who had given Pleasant control of the family's finances. Mary Ellen was understandably taken aback by accusations of being unfit to manage the affairs that she had expertly handled for so many years. Additionally, she had housed the entire Bell family, including six children all that time.

Every aspect of Pleasant's finances and personal relationships with the Bells became public knowledge during the trial, thanks to reporters all too happy to drag her name through the mud once again. In the end Pleasant's facade as the Bell's servant had been chipped away; the judge ruled that such a lowly status should preclude her from any fiduciary management for the family.

Since many of Pleasant's holdings had been commingled with those of Thomas Bell for so long, it was difficult to separate and prove her rightful share. She had done such a good job of hiding her wealth over the years that in the end, it was nearly impossible to untangle the secret partnerships. Her long-standing relationship with Teresa Bell and her family disintegrated through the trial to disengage Mary Ellen Pleasant from overseeing the Bell's finances. Their personal relationships were understandably strained, and Pleasant was forced out of her stately mansion. Mary Ellen felt betrayed by Teresa Bell's actions.

In November 1903, Mary Ellen Pleasant, who was in declining health, was invited to live with friends Lyman and Olive Sherwood. She died at their home on Filbert Street in San Francisco on January 11, 1904, at the age of eighty-five. Following a lifetime of absurd allegations, personal attacks, and the betrayal of those she employed and befriended—all played out in a public forum—she left an estate of $10,000, which failed to come even close to representing her financial accomplishments. She left the money to Sam Davis of Carson City, Nevada, a friend who had stood by her.

Mary Ellen Pleasant was buried in Tulocay Cemetery in Napa Valley along with other well-known pioneer leaders and prominent citizens. Her commitment to those who fought valiantly for freedom was evidenced in her dying wish. She had only one request—that the inscription on her headstone make note of her association with radical abolitionist John Brown. The epitaph reads MARY ELLEN PLEASANT—MOTHER OF CIVIL RIGHTS IN CALIFORNIA—1812–1904—SHE WAS A FRIEND OF JOHN BROWN.

Mary Ellen Pleasant's house on Webster Street in San Francisco was torn down in 1964 to build a dental school. Demolished, too, was the Victorian mansion on Octavia and Bush, where today a commemorative plaque has been placed at the site by the African-American Historical and Cultural Society. That and several eucalyptus trees nearby are all the physical evidence that remains to remind people of her grand Mystery House and her numerous contributions to the welfare of blacks in San Francisco, but her legend lives on.

February 10 is recognized as Mary Ellen Pleasant Day in San Francisco. Abolitionist, entrepreneur, and successful venture capitalist, she was one of the most enterprising—and enigmatic—black women of the nineteenth century. For more than fifty years, she helped shape the economy of one of America's greatest cities while doing all she could to better her race. While she despised being referred to as "mammy" later in life, she did hide behind that mask at times when it served her best. The complexity of her character is exemplified in such duplicity. Yet in her mind she was simply working her way around the confines of white society.

Like Mother, Like Daughter

Elizabeth Thorn Scott Flood

WHEN THE CHILDREN SPOTTED THE MIDWIFE making her way up the dusty road, they began jumping up and down in joyful anticipation. With the impending arrival of their new sibling, they had been scooted outside the house and told to stay out. The youngsters excitedly ran to hurry the old woman along as she made her way to their small home on East Fifteenth Street in Oakland, California. They begged her to hurry: This child was clearly not going to waste any time making an entrance into the world.

Soon enough after the arrival of the midwife, the loud cries of the newborn pierced the air. Miss Lydia Flood had announced her arrival on a beautiful spring day on June 9, 1862. Her mother, thirty-four-year-old Elizabeth Thorn Scott Flood, sat up in bed as best she could. As she held her only daughter gently in her arms, the four older boys gathered around to see what the tiny infant was screaming about. Elizabeth smiled a sweet smile. This was one young lady whose cries were going to be heard in the world, and Elizabeth immediately recognized the similarity between her daughter and herself.

Life in California had been nothing like what Elizabeth Thorn Scott had foreseen. She and her late husband, Joseph

Scott, had been born free and had the privilege of excellent educations in New Bedford, Massachusetts. With high hopes and adventuresome spirits, they had left for San Francisco by way of Panama, presumably lured west during the gold rush. In 1852 they had settled with their California-born son in Hangtown (Placerville) in El Dorado County, where Joseph was mining for gold. After becoming widowed, however, Elizabeth felt that such a rough-and-rowdy town was not the place for a single mother to raise a son. Looking for better opportunities, she bravely set out on her own.

Sacramento was one of the larger cities in the West and was said to have a sizable black community. She decided to see what possibilities were there. Elizabeth's passion in life was the attainment of education, and she found an outlet for her passions among the community of blacks who had gone west in search of gold and a better life. These pioneer families in California lucky enough to come in contact with Elizabeth would benefit from her trailblazing efforts.

By the 1850s education of the races in the West was segregated not by law, but by tradition. Elizabeth Thorn Scott saw the inequality in education because of segregation soon after arriving in Sacramento. It did not anger her as much as it lit a fire in her. In speaking with other pioneer parents, she found that they, too, longed for their children to be educated. They were eager to give their children every opportunity to succeed.

St. Andrew's Church in Sacramento, established in 1850, was the first African Methodist Episcopal (AME) church on the Pacific coast. It was the first to start a Sunday school for its members. Ten days later Elizabeth Thorn Scott decided to open a school for nonwhites. She realized that establishing religious

Elizabeth Thorn Scott Flood
COURTESY AFRICAN AMERICAN MUSEUM AND LIBRARY, OAKLAND (AAMLO)

institutions brought communities together and that Sunday schools were the precursors to academic schools.

Purchasing a school for the prospective students in Sacramento was cost-prohibitive for pioneer families, who worked hard just to make ends meet. However, Elizabeth's own home on Second Street between M and N Streets was centrally located and large enough for the task; so on May 29, 1854, at the age of twenty-six, Elizabeth opened her home. It was to be the first private "colored" school in town.

Fourteen students came through Elizabeth's front door, not all of them children. There were Lauretta J. Bryson, Mrs. Mary

Ann Burns, George Booth, Edward Yantes, Laura M. Luckett, Richard Brown, Thomas Allen, Cornelius Campbell, George Waters, Ruebin Johnson, Alice Mitchell, Chesterfield Woodson, Abraham Goodlow, and Frederick Sparrow. Elizabeth's pupils ranged in age from four to twenty-nine, and all looked to her with eyes hungry for knowledge.

Elizabeth was determined that her students would not be denied an education no matter what the barriers. In nine weeks' time she could see their progress, as well as a growing interest in her school. On August 7, 1854, their small community had organized to establish Sacramento's first public school. It was to be held in the basement of St. Andrew's Church on Seventh Street, and all fourteen students were transferred to the new location. The doors of Elizabeth's new school were open to African Americans as well as Mongolians and Native Americans. Each student's family paid tuition of $1.00 per week.

A school committee comprising one woman and seven men formed to oversee the school and gather what supplies Elizabeth requested. It was decided that as teacher she would be paid by subscription, with each family contributing to her monthly salary of $50. Out of this came all the materials that the students would need—slates, chalk, paper, pencils, ink, pens, and, of course, textbooks.

Fledgling black pioneer communities were finding that the best way to promote their own welfare was to form their own institutions, whether churches, social groups, or schools. By 1849 the California constitutional convention decided to establish a state school fund. These monies would be obtained from taxation and the sale or rental of public lands. As Elizabeth sadly knew, however, racial discrimination had reared its ugly head out West, and local school boards prevented black schools from receiving any funds.

Elizabeth found that pioneers who were concerned about the education of their youth were eager to support schools. State legislatures realized that these private and parochial schools often evolved into public facilities. To encourage this trend, the legislature allocated state monies to such schools on the basis of pupil attendance. At first it might have seemed like good news for Elizabeth's school, but it wasn't for long. The financial support lasted only a few short years, as opposition to public funds for private schools won out and funding was curtailed in 1855.

Elizabeth Thorn Scott became even more determined to help African Americans elevate their station in life through education. Her goal was to create such opportunities for minorities. The establishment of Colored State Conventions allowed for an organized base from which to fight discrimination. It was one of the best ways in which to present a unified front in demanding the right to testify in court, suffrage, and equality in education. Representatives from ten counties in the state first convened at St. Andrew's Church in November 1855. Leaders from all fields flocked to the conventions to show their support for equal opportunities for all people. It is thought that Elizabeth Thorn Scott met her second husband, Isaac Flood, at one of the Colored Conventions held there.

Isaac Flood did not have the same upbringing as Elizabeth. He was twelve years her senior and had been born as a slave in South Carolina. When he was twenty-two years old, he was given his freedom and came to California by ship in 1849. Like Elizabeth, Isaac also had lived in El Dorado County while searching for gold. By the early 1850s he had moved to Brooklyn, California, a small town on the east side of Oakland, where he lived with his son. He worked as a laborer and had many civic and social concerns for his people. This shared passion caught Elizabeth's eye, and in 1855 the two were married.

Elizabeth Thorn Scott Flood retired from teaching after her marriage. She and her son moved with her husband and his son to the community of Brooklyn. This move left her school at St. Andrew's Church without a teacher for a while. But on April 20, 1855, it was reopened when a very capable replacement was found. Jeremiah B. Sanderson, also from New Bedford, Massachusetts, agreed to carry the torch Elizabeth had lit.

Like Mrs. Flood, Mr. Sanderson found that the subscription from the families of the thirty children did not provide the means for an education equal to that of the white public schools. By comparison even the teacher salaries were unequal. A white public-school teacher's salary was $1,000 compared to $600 for a black private-school teacher. Sanderson was instrumental in getting the Sacramento Board of Education to open a public school for nonwhites. Throughout his career he would come to be known as the father of schools for nonwhite children in California.

Elizabeth Thorn Scott Flood, of course, is recognized as the mother of schools for children of color in California. She was a pioneer in the truest sense of the word. By leading the battle to better the plight of her own people and that of other minorities, she paved the way for public education in the state. Other communities followed suit, and schools opened in such Northern California towns as Marysville, Grass Valley, Red Bluff, and Chico.

Yet Elizabeth wasn't satisfied. After arriving in San Francisco's East Bay area, which encompassed the small communities of Brooklyn and Oakland, she realized that there was much work to be done. Oakland was founded in 1852 in a picturesque area, with mountains and beautiful oak trees dotting the landscape. Elizabeth saw the possibility of the two adjacent black communities prospering, but realized that their future was the children and their schooling was of utmost importance.

In 1856 Elizabeth gave birth to a son, George Francis Flood, said to be the first black baby born in Alameda County. Four years earlier the census showed only eighteen people living in Oakland, but more and more people were moving to the area. The cost of living was less than that of San Francisco, and employment opportunities were growing more plentiful as black businesses relocated to the area. A particular impetus was the location of the transcontinental railroad's terminus in Oakland. With families came children, and Elizabeth set off on a campaign to solicit support for another school.

In 1857 Elizabeth Thorn Scott Flood opened a school in her home on 1334 East Fifteenth Avenue in Brooklyn. This was the first private black school in the Oakland area and was open to all minorities. Members of the black community supported this effort, paying tuition on top of paying taxes for the public schools from which their children were barred. The burden was great, but their shared vision of uplifting their race gave them a oneness of purpose.

Elizabeth Flood's goal was to design her school to be competitive with the white public schools. In the 1850s, exemplary school systems were found in New York, Ohio, and New England. The California legislature was attempting to create comparable facilities. Fortunately, since Elizabeth had been educated in the East, she was very familiar with curricular requirements.

By 1860 the state board of education decided to adopt textbooks statewide. While Elizabeth surely did not have the funding to purchase textbooks for all her students, she did prepare a thorough curriculum for them. She began with the basics, but her expectations were high. To be respected as having received a quality education, her students would have to exceed the level of competence their white peers achieved. Her main curriculum would include the three R's—reading, writing, and arithmetic— as well as geography, spelling, grammar, elocution, U.S. history, general science, and vocal music.

It was in 1862 that Elizabeth's daughter, Lydia Flood, was born. She and her husband now had five children to raise, and their goal was to see that they had every opportunity to succeed in life. The children attended Elizabeth's school and saw first-hand the sacrifices and struggles that had to be overcome in order to enjoy the privilege of a quality education. Elizabeth inevitably instilled into her young daughter, Lydia, a sense of the value of an education.

Besides raising a family, teaching, and being a pioneer in education, Elizabeth realized that religious institutions were needed for communities to grow. The year after she started her private school in Oakland, therefore, she and Isaac, along with some other leaders, organized Oakland's first black church. It began as a mission in 1858; without a sitting pastor or a building, members opened their homes for services. In 1863 this mission Elizabeth helped start became the Shiloh AME Church, and the Floods were among the trustees. This church did exactly what Elizabeth had known it would do: It led the way for the growth of other religious and secular institutions.

Elizabeth's school was about to undergo a change that surely made her proud. In 1863 the Shiloh AME Church purchased the abandoned Carpentier School House, which had been built in

1853 as a white public school. The church paid $50 for the building with its redwood clapboard sides and shingled roof. They put $30 down with a balance of 2 percent per month. It was quite an undertaking to move the building to its new location on Seventh Street and Market. The small 22-by-38-foot room served as both chapel and schoolroom. Elizabeth could stand on the small covered porch watching her students, including her own children, flock to her new school as the bell in the belfry was rung to announce the commencement of the day's lessons. This school stayed open for a total of ten years, serving the youth of Oakland.

Elizabeth Thorn Scott Flood lived to see changes made by the legislature that widened the door she had opened for minority students. The revised School Law of 1866 did not admit nonwhite children to the public schools, but it did provide separate public schools to be established for black children if there were ten or more students. (One such school was established in Brooklyn in 1867 in the old Manning House.) If there were fewer than ten children, the black students could attend white schools.

In 1867 Elizabeth Thorn Scott Flood died unexpectedly at the young age of thirty-nine. Her children attended the public school in Brooklyn and went on to further their education as schools were opened to them. Elizabeth's husband, Isaac, continued their quest for equal education for all children. He petitioned the Oakland School Board in 1871 to accept minority children based on the passage of the Fourteenth and Fifteenth Amendments, which superseded the state's current discriminatory laws. Elizabeth would have been very proud to see that her trailblazing work did indeed open the doors for equal opportunity.

In 1872 Brooklyn admitted minority children into its schools, and shortly thereafter the Oakland School Board voted five to two to do the same. Elizabeth's daughter, Lydia, was among the first students to attend Oakland's integrated public school, the old John Swett School. Still, what would likely have pleased her the most were two rulings made by the legislature: In 1875 the black schools were closed, and in 1880 integrated schools became the law in California. At long last Elizabeth's goal was attained: Public school doors were open to everyone regardless of race, color, or creed.

Lydia Flood reaped the benefits of a good education. She went on to become an outspoken champion of women's rights and worked for the betterment of her race in California, South America, Mexico, and the West Indies. She furthered her education, started her own business, married, and continued to promote equality for all. Lydia Flood Jackson spoke at the California State Woman's Convention in 1918 in favor of suffrage. She held several officer positions in the California State Association of Colored Women's Clubs, demanding the right to vote for women.

What her mother, Elizabeth, could never have foreseen was that Lydia would be present at the eightieth anniversary of the Shiloh AME Church she had helped found. The congregation was thrilled to have their oldest living member address them. Lydia never failed to mention the accomplishments of her mother, who had opened the doors for countless others both in education and religion. The Shiloh AME Church, now known as the First African Methodist Episcopal Church, still exists in Oakland.

For 101 years Lydia Flood cried out against the injustices that impeded her race. Like her mother she fought the uphill battle for equality and championed educational rights. Fortunately, Lydia Flood lived to see the gates of opportunity begin to open. By 1880 black students were graduating from universities and colleges with honors and awards. Elizabeth Thorn Scott Flood had known all along that all black students needed to succeed was the opportunity to do so.

THE VOICE OF REASON
Susie Revels Cayton

SUSIE SUMNER REVELS'S LONG-DISTANCE correspondence with Horace Roscoe Cayton began innocently enough. It started with her transcribing the letters her father dictated to Mr. Cayton and then gradually progressed into more personal communications. The last thing Susie Revels had expected from the exchange of letters with a man eleven years her senior was a marriage proposal, but when it happened, it seemed a perfect fit.

Susie had known Cayton since 1881, when she was eleven. At the time Susie's father, the Reverend Hiram Revels, a minister in the African Methodist Episcopal Church, was a teacher as well as the first president of Alcorn College in Mississippi. Susie's older sister, Lillie, was being courted by none other than Mr. Cayton, both of whom attended Alcorn College. While the two collegians sat sparking on the front-porch swing, young Susie amused herself on the lawn. When Mr. Cayton decided to head West after graduation in search of better opportunities, Susie most likely never gave him another thought.

Years later Horace Cayton had ended up in Seattle, where he started a newspaper, the *Seattle Republican,* in 1894. He had kept in touch with the Revels family after leaving Mississippi and sent copies of his newspaper back to the reverend. Though there was no longer a romantic interest between him and the elder Revels daughter, perhaps he wanted the esteemed ex-senator and professor to see that he had made something of himself. Susie's father would read the newspapers and dictate replies to Horace Cayton. It was after taking the dictation that Susie added some family news at the end of the letters. Over the course of a few years, she and Horace Cayton began corresponding regularly. This grew into an exchange of ideas and, ultimately, a life together.

Susie Sumner Revels was born in 1870, the year her father took office in Washington, D.C. The Reverend Hiram Revels had been elected by the Mississippi legislature as U.S. senator. Being the first African American to hold such a position earned him a prestigious place in the history of the nation. It would also open doors of opportunity for Susie.

Both her parents had been free as far back as they could remember. Her mother, Phoebe Bass Revels, was an educated Quaker woman. Her father, who held office during the Reconstruction era, was an outspoken opponent of racial segregation. They had high expectations for their children.

Susie Sumner Revels was named for a family friend, Republican Senator Charles Sumner, an ardent abolitionist. She came to take the ideals of both her father and her namesake to heart. They all shared a passion for racial equality, enlightenment, and advancement of the oppressed. By a young age these goals were firmly ingrained and no doubt paved the way for Susie to one day become a leading citizen and one of Seattle's most influential black pioneers.

Susie was an exceptionally bright young girl full of personality. She and her five sisters led a rather privileged life for their time. They were fortunate to be exposed to such an intellectually

Susie Revels Cayton
SEATTLE REPUBLICAN PHOTO

stimulating environment as Mississippi's Alcorn University, located 80 miles southwest of the capital, Jackson. Susie had a curious mind, a thirst for knowledge that seemed insatiable, and a keen intellect. Living near a college campus environment helped her budding talent for writing to evolve.

Tragedy befell the Revels family in 1879 when Susie was just nine years old. A yellow fever epidemic hit their town of Holly Springs. Better than 10 percent of the town's 3,500 residents died, including Susie's newly married sister, Emma. Another sister, Maggie, suffered the same fate not long after.

When Susie was twelve, her father retired from Alcorn and accepted a teaching position at Rust College in Holly Springs, Mississippi. Susie continued her education at the town's normal school (what today would be called a teachers college). Becoming a teacher was a natural for Susie, with her love for imparting knowledge. At sixteen she began teaching at several schools while continuing her education at Rust College. After graduation Susie went on to teach at the college just like her father.

Through her correspondence with Horace Cayton in her mid-twenties, Susie found someone with whom she could identify—a man who shared not only her own ideals, but also the zeal and enthusiasm that prompted her to make a difference in the world. Susie fervently believed in peaceful relations among all races, equal opportunities for jobs and education, social outreach, and general uplift of the black race. She was determined to work for justice.

Susie admired Horace's drive and strong sense of right and wrong. The articulate, outspoken young editor embraced the hopefulness of the Reconstruction era yet understood that the South did not hold the answer for upwardly mobile black youth. Susie agreed that the Pacific Northwest seemed to hold less prejudice and offer more opportunities for black people who wanted to work for change. When thirty-seven-year-old Horace Cayton wrote and asked for twenty-six-year-old Susie's hand in marriage, she accepted. He seemed to be going places, and that was just what Susie intended to do herself.

There is every reason to believe that the Reverend Hiram Revels approved of the ambitious Cayton, for they shared many of the same ideals. Revels knew that his future son-in-law appreciated his daughter for her own ideas and recognized her abilities. For months that year Susie had been writing stories that Horace published in his newspaper. In the 1896 New Year's edition of the *Seattle Republican,* there appeared an article by Miss Susan Sumner Revels concerning Booker T. Washington and the Atlanta Exposition, which was well received. Horace Cayton publicly praised her contributions, stating for his readership, "She gives every evidence of becoming a very forcible and effective writer and seems especially adapted to fiction and verse."

Upon approval of their engagement, the soon-to-be Mrs. Horace Cayton chose to move to the Northwest. Miss Revels took a train to Seattle, where her fiancé respectfully found living arrangements for her until the time of their wedding. She was a tall, pretty woman with a gentle, warm demeanor who exuded grace and class. Her marriage to Horace would bring him prestige.

July 12, 1896, was a beautiful summer day for the couple to exchange their vows. The wedding was held at the Seattle home of Mr. A. J. T. Edwards. The Reverend Shanklin of the First Methodist Episcopal Church officiated. Two families with distinctly different backgrounds, yet who shared common bonds, were united in marriage.

Both the Revels and Caytons had a mixed racial ancestry. Unlike Susie's family, though, Horace traced his heritage to slavery. Never quite certain of his parentage, Horace's father, or stepfather, and his mother raised him on a plantation for the first six years of his life. It wasn't until the end of the Civil War that the Caytons were freed. Susie would come to know of the gruesome experiences that the elder Cayton had as a slave. Though she could not personally identify with slavery, she knew that it was a part of her husband and that their children would have a heritage both slave and free.

Susie had much in common with her husband, however. Both were college-educated intellectuals with interests in journalism and backgrounds in teaching and writing. They both came from Christian households with strong morals, and both knew the importance of hard work. They shared a passion for justice, and their contributions would move Seattle toward racial equality.

The fact that white supremacist southerners were generally Democrats caused many blacks, including Susie Revels Cayton and her husband, to identify with Lincoln's Republican Party, and the very Republican Mr. and Mrs. Horace Cayton were eager to make a life for themselves in Seattle, which in the latter half of the nineteenth century was known as a place where blacks were given a fair shake. There were no Black Laws restricting their rights, as was the case in Oregon. Seattle had a reputation as being less prejudiced than other areas of the country. It was a place where Susie believed that her hopes and dreams might be realized. For that, no road was too long.

The *Seattle Republican,* which Horace Cayton founded, was the second black newspaper in Seattle. In a ten-year period prior to 1901, a total of seven black weekly newspapers appeared in town. Most were strongly partisan, but all strove to improve the situation for blacks in society. The *Republican* was a biracial newspaper intended for both a black and white readership. Several years after the couple married, their newspaper became very prosperous. Susie Cayton was acknowledged publicly by her husband as the force behind its success. The *Seattle Republican* was clearly Republican in its bent, and at every chance it sought to show the black race in a good light. The Caytons publicized those participating in acts of community service, civic responsibility, or any accomplishment of note.

Susie had begun writing around the age of ten. Several of her stories from that period exist today, such as "Licker" and "The Storm." Her love of writing continued her whole life, and she had a genuine flair for the pen. Besides helping to run the *Republican,* Susie was a regular contributor. She had studied both journalism and nursing in college, but her love was journalism. Besides the Caytons' own newspaper, her stories appeared in the *Seattle Post-Intelligencer,* a white newspaper. Its June 3, 1900 issue ran a piece titled "Sallie the Egg-Woman," an essay about the mysterious doings of a devoted elderly black woman caring for a demented young woman in her charge. The piece clearly showcased Susie's talent and was apparently well received by the paper's readership. Other newspapers commented favorably on her writing as well.

In 1900 Susie Revels Cayton became associate editor of the *Seattle Republican.* The paper's masthead prominently displayed her name and the title she so richly deserved. Susie contributed articles, editorials, and short stories. The journal touted that it was the "only paper in the Northwest successfully edited by a Negro." The Caytons could attribute its success to keeping to the four R's: "Always Regular, Readable, Reliable, Republican." Susie's work also earned the praise of the *Seattle Times,* a white newspaper. Her husband publicly acknowledged her contribution to the success of their newspaper by printing "the associate hereof and likewise life partner of the editor has more than borne her part . . . All honor is due to such women."

The Caytons were one of the most prominent, wealthy, and respected black families in Seattle. In 1903 Susie and her family moved to the prestigious Capitol Hill, where they lived in an eight-room two-story home with a carriage house. She gave birth to two sons, one in 1903 and another in 1907, while living at 518 Fourteenth Avenue. Susie was part of the elite black middle class living in an affluent white neighborhood.

The small group of upper-class blacks was always busy planning social get-togethers such as picnics, sightseeing trips, barbecues, dinner parties, and balls. Other members of black society did the same, even if on a much reduced scale. Family and fellowship bonded people together.

While her husband combined politics and journalism to make a living, Susie preferred community outreach to complement her love of journalism. As a college-educated newspaper editor, her visibility enabled her to become a leader in social and civic circles. She supported cultural events and encouraged participation. Susie was a proponent of active community life, joining organizations and inspiring others to do the same. She was especially active in the Sunday Forum, an all-black group formed to promote discussion of issues of concern within their community. Their unified front carried clout. If businesses that blacks patronized refused them employment, for instance, they could threaten to withdraw their support until the situation was rectified. Susie was a participant and speaker at this bimonthly club, which met over a four-year period.

Susie was also a founding member of the Dorcas Club, a charity group in which she held several leadership roles. At one point she saw a need for black girls to have black baby dolls rather than white ones and went about seeing to the change.

What Susie Revels Cayton recognized was the importance of social uplift. She also realized the value of an education in helping to bring families out of poverty. Ignorance, she knew, kept black women down. Self-esteem was essential for black women after the demoralizing experiences of the slavery era, which had ended for many as recently as 1865. The women Susie knew were either former slaves or children of such. Susie tried to help lift those women who were trying desperately to distance themselves from their pasts.

Besides keeping their family unit intact, black women had to offer financial support—their husbands typically could only find low-paying jobs. Susie wanted employment opportunities for these women other than as domestics or laundresses. Equally important, she wanted them to have their self-respect. She found that most women believed they might never see their own hopes and aspirations realized, but believed that their children's lives and opportunities might be much improved.

Susie was able to balance working outside the home at the paper and her social outreach as well as raising her children. She would have five children, three girls and two boys, born over the space of seventeen years in Seattle. Though the children were just one generation removed from slavery, they were expected to be leaders in society: Service and achievement were paramount. Susie's high expectations for her own children were seen in her insistence in having them use standard English. They were admonished to show the best of manners at all times to improve the image of blacks. They were expected to be a credit to their race. For a while Susie and her family seemed to be living the American dream, in which hard work secured success and civic involvement assured acceptance.

However, as racial unrest intensified in Seattle, Susie saw their world begin to crumble. The changing social climate certainly contributed to the decline of the *Seattle Republican* in 1909. Susie stood by and watched as her husband lost a legal battle after he'd been refused service in a restaurant. The couple was accused, too, of causing their neighborhood's real estate value to depreciate. It was further proof that they were losing their respect and standing in the white community. After all their work to promote harmony, it was disheartening to see the color line return to prominence as it was across the country. The financial losses that Susie's family suffered as a result reduced their station in life.

In 1909, after six years of living in the enviable Capitol Hill, the Caytons were forced to move—the first of several relocations. They lived in a small house near The Laurel, a twenty-three-room boarding house that they owned and operated on Twenty-second Avenue South. Susie had long since let go the Japanese servant and Swedish maid whom they'd employed. Some real estate investments that did not pan out depleted their savings, as did civil lawsuits Horace was involved in. Susie did all she could to hold the family together and help make ends meet. By then her children were twelve, eight, six, and two years old (she would give birth to their fifth child, a daughter, in 1914). Still the *Seattle Republican* struggled to survive as businesses pulled their advertisements and subscriptions decreased.

The policy of the *Seattle Republican* had been to work through difficulties between the races by "full and free discussion of them." But tackling sensitive race issues openly in the paper was not well received. Between 1890 and 1900 more than 1,200 lynchings took place in the Deep South, and the Caytons' insistence on publishing accounts of these horrific acts, as well as rapes of black women and more, offended their white readership. On

May 13, 1913, the last edition of the *Seattle Republican* was printed. It had run for nineteen years.

After the paper failed, Susie saw her husband lose his position of influence in the white Republican machine that he had long supported. Over the years she had watched her husband bring distress to her family through printing his outspoken views, name-calling, and refusal to just sit back and take it. She supported her family when some of these causes left him in jail, as unjust as the arrests were. At times she was frightened for her life and the lives of her children, but she endured their reversal of fortune and status with grace under pressure.

In 1916 Susie and Horace had enough money to start another newspaper, *Cayton's Weekly*. Fighting back against discrimination, the paper was distinctly aimed at a black circulation. It continued to report atrocities committed against blacks to incite people to action. As a contributing editor of *Cayton's Weekly,* Susie did not always agree with the degree to which her husband reported such injustices, but she sympathized with his conviction. Conversely, the paper ran stories of accomplishments and contributions of blacks to society in order promote a good image of the race. The paper ran until late 1920 and was soon replaced by *Cayton's Monthly*. Regrettably, that had a run of just two issues.

In 1919 the couple suffered another personal loss: Their eldest daughter died. At age forty-nine Susie became the guardian of her twelve-month-old granddaughter, Susan, and raised her as her own child.

While Susie's goals remained the same as her husband's, she increasingly found the old means of achieving these goals futile. She felt that her husband was out of touch with the average black person. Even when circumstances related to the Great Depression of 1929 up through the early 1940s put them on the edge of poverty, Horace remained loyal to what he knew. In truth blacks still had their "place," even in Seattle. When the repercussions of the Depression soundly hit the black community, lack of employment opportunities and social restrictions were a reality. Even menial jobs were hard to find as unemployment exploded. Susie found it impossible to re-enter the workforce in 1919 as a college-educated woman. The only jobs available were well beneath her, and even those went to white folks. The doors of opportunity were closed—and that opened Susie's mind to a whole new way of thinking.

Susie Revels Cayton came to identify with the working class and poor of all races in Seattle. Her goal was to promote the welfare of all who were struggling to survive. Around age sixty-five, Susie Revels Cayton became politically active. She believed that there would be less racial discrimination in a socialist society. Consequently she took after her youngest son and joined the Communist Party. This strongly differed from the views held by her husband, whom she witnessed become increasingly depressed after spending a lifetime exhausting avenues for change.

Susie's alliance with the Communist Party, on the other hand, made her feel hopeful. Through her social activism she helped to enact change. She involved herself with countless causes and kept a hectic agenda despite her age and declining health. She had developed friendships with political activists and radical intellectuals such as famed speaker and actor Paul Robeson as well as poet Langston Hughes, both of whom shared her interest in social issues.

Susie cared for her husband, Horace, as his health failed him. She bolstered his spirits when he failed to find a publisher for his autobiography. He died in 1940 at age eighty-one. Susie spread his ashes in Puget Sound, lovingly saying farewell to a life partner with whom she may not have always agreed, but whom she greatly admired.

Susie Revels Cayton maintained a busy schedule, keeping active in the Communist Party until her health failed her. In early 1942 her children moved her to Chicago. There friends called upon her; Paul Robeson and Langston Hughes sought her out for lively political discussions. Even her son's friend, the author Richard Wright, who himself had ties with Communist Party ideology, was interested in hearing her ideas on progressive means to accomplish equal protection under the law for all. Social activism seemed to be her calling.

On July 28, 1943, Susie Sumner Revels Cayton died from advancing age in conjunction with the effects of diabetes. She was seventy-four. As with her husband, her ashes were scattered in Puget Sound. She and Horace came together and pulled apart, but always remained committed to the betterment of their race.

Susie Revels Cayton was an anomaly. At a time when blacks had very little education, she was highly educated. She was able to fulfill her dreams in becoming an associate editor of a successful newspaper as well as an author of some note. She worked diligently for equality envisioning a time when blacks and whites would live in peace and harmony.

Perhaps her greatest contribution, though, was the legacy that she left behind in her children. They all knew from whence they came, and their lives were uniquely defined by the bequest that they inherited. A Cayton was expected to make a significant contribution to society by working for the betterment of the race, fighting segregation, or participating in the general uplift of the oppressed.

The legacy that the Cayton descendants inherited at times put them in the spotlight. They achieved varying degrees of success in various fields, some in a very private way, and others through public service. Some struggled to find their own identity as black people in a society often unwilling to accept them, leaving them embittered. Others met with success and fulfillment.

Today the Cayton Scholarship, established in 1992, honors the contributions of Seattle's pioneer journalists. It is available to minority college students studying public relations or communications in the state of Washington.

BIBLIOGRAPHY

Books

Abajian, James de T. *Blacks in Selected Newspapers, Censuses and Other Sources: An Index to Name and Subjects.* Boston: G. K. Hall, 1985.

Anderson, Martha. *Black Pioneers of the Northwest 1800–1918.* S.I.: s.n., 1980.

Aptheker, Bettina. *Woman's Legacy Essays on Race, Sex, and Class in American History.* Amherst: University of Massachusetts Press, 1982.

Athearn, Robert G. *In Search of Canaan Black Migration to Kansas 1879–80.* Lawrence: Regents Press of Kansas, 1978.

Baker, Roger. *Clara: An Ex-Slave in Gold Rush Colorado.* Central City, Colo.: Black Hawk Publishing, 2003.

Barrett, Ivan J. *Heroic Mormon Women.* American Fork, Utah: Covenant Communications, 1991.

Beasley, Delilah L. *The Negro Trailblazers of California.* New York: G. K. Hall, 1919.

Billington, Monroe Lee, and Roger D. Hardaway. *African Americans on the Western Frontier.* Niwot: University Press of Colorado, 1998.

Bolden, Tonya. *The Book of African-American Women.* Holbrook, Mass.: Adams Media, 1996.

Bontemps, Anna, and Jack Conroy. *Anyplace but Here.* New York: Hill and Wang, 1966.

Brooks, Juanita, editor. *On the Mormon Frontier: The Diary of Hosea Stout 1844–1861.* Salt Lake City: University of Utah Press, 1964.

Brown, Marion. *Pickles and Preserves*. Chapel Hill: University of North Carolina Press, 2002.

Bunch, Lonnie III. *Black Angelenos: The African American in Los Angeles, 1850–1950*. Los Angeles, 1989.

Carter, Kate B. *Our Pioneer Heritage*. Salt Lake City: Daughters of Utah Pioneers, 1965.

Collins, Gail. *America's Women: 400 Years of Dolls, Drudges, Helpmates, and Heroines*. New York: William Morrow, 2003.

Crouchett, Lawrence P., Lonnie G. Bunch III, and Martha Kendall Winnacker. *Visions toward Tomorrow: The History of the East Bay Afro-American Community 1852–1977*. Oakland: Northern California Center for Afro-American History and Life, 1989.

Diaz, Ed, comp. and ed. *Horace Roscoe Cayton Selected Writings*. Volume 1 and 2. Seattle: Bridgewater-Collins, 2002.

_____. *Stories by Cayton: Short Stories by Susie Revels Cayton, a Seattle Pioneer*. Seattle: Bridgewater-Collins, 2002.

Drotning, Philip T. *A Guide to Negro History in America*. Garden City, N.Y.: Doubleday, 1968.

Durham, Philip, and Everett L. Jones. *The Negro Cowboys*. New York: Dodd, Mead, 1965.

Edwords, Clarence E. *Bohemian San Francisco: Its Restaurants and Their Most Famous Recipes—The Elegant Art of Dining*. San Francisco: Paul Elder, 1914.

Empak Series. *A Salute to Historic Black Women*. Chicago: Empak Publishing, 1984.

———. *Historic Black Pioneers*. Chicago: Empak Enterprises, 1990.

———. *A Gift of Heritage: A Salute to Black Pioneers.* Chicago: Empak Publishing, 1996.

Falk, Charles J. *The Development and Organization of Education in California.* New York: Harcourt, Brace & World, 1968.

Fisher, Abby. *What Mrs. Fisher Knows about Old Southern Cooking, Soups, Pickles, Preserves, Etc.* San Francisco: Women's Co-operative Printing Office, 1881.

———. *What Mrs. Fisher Knows about Old Southern Cooking, Soups, Pickles, Preserves, Etc. Facsimile edition, with historical notes by Karen Hess.* Bedford, Mass.: Applewood Books, 1995.

Glozer, Liselotte F., and William Glozer. *California in the Kitchen: An Essay Upon, and a Check List of California Imprints in the Field of Gastronomy from 1870(?)–1932.* Privately printed, 1960.

Goode, Kenneth G. *California's Black Pioneers: A Brief Historical Survey.* Santa Barbara: McNally & Loftin, 1974.

Hall, Frank. *History of the Statehood of Colorado for the Rocky Mountain Historical Society.* Chicago: Blakely Printing, 1889.

Hambleton, Madison D. *Journal Church Emigration Book,* Vol. I. Utah: Salt Lake Valley Emigration Census, 1847.

Hayden, Dolores. *The Power of Place: Urban Landscapes as Public History.* Cambridge, Mass.: MIT Press, 1995.

Hine, Darlene Clark. *Black Women in America: An Historical Encyclopedia.* Bloomington: Indiana University Press, 1994.

———. *Black Women in American History from Colonial Times through the Nineteenth Century.* Brooklyn, N.Y.: Carlson Publishing, 1990.

Hirsch, E. D. Jr., Joseph F. Kett, and James Trefil. *The Dictionary of Cultural Literacy*. Boston: Houghton Mifflin, 1988.

Hobbs, Richard S. *The Cayton Legacy: An African American Family*. Pullman: Washington State University Press, 2002.

———. *The Cayton Legacy: Two Generations of a Black Family 1859–1976*. Ann Arbor, Mich.: University Microfilms International, 1989.

Hoobler, Dorothy, and Thomas Hoobler. *The African American Family Album*. New York: Oxford University Press, 1995.

Hudson, Lynn M. *The Making of "Mammy" Pleasant: A Black Entrepreneur in Nineteenth-Century San Francisco*. Urbana and Chicago: University of Illinois Press, 2003.

International Society of the Daughters of Utah Pioneers. *Pioneer Women of Faith and Fortitude*. 4 volumes. Salt Lake City: Publishers Press, 1998.

Jackson, George. *Black Woman Makers of History*. Sacramento: Fong & Fong, 1977.

Katz, William Lorenz. *Black People Who Made the Old West*. New York: Thomas Y. Crowell, 1977.

———. *The Black West: A Documentary and Pictorial History of the African American Role in the Westward Expansion of the United States*. New York: Simon & Schuster, 1996.

———. *Eyewitness: A Living Documentary of the African American Contribution to American History*. New York: Simon & Schuster, 1995.

———. *Black Women of the Old West*. New York: Atheneum Books for Young Readers, 1995.

Ketchum, Liza. *Into a New Country: Eight Remarkable Women of the West*. Boston: Little, Brown, 2000.

Lehman, Jeffrey. *The African American Almanac*. Detroit: Thomson Gale, 2003.

Levenson, Roger. *Women in Printing: Northern California, 1857–1890*. Santa Barbara: Capra Press, 1994.

Lowery, Linda. *One More Valley, One More Hill: The Story of Aunt Clara Brown*. New York: Random House, 2002.

Marriott, Barbara. *Annie's Guests: Tales from a Frontier Hotel*. Tucson: Catymatt Productions, 2002.

Maruyama, Susan J. *Perseverance: African Americans Voices of Triumph*. Alexandria, Va.: Time Life Books, 1993.

McLagan, Elizabeth. *A Peculiar Paradise: A History of Blacks in Oregon, 1788–1940*. The Oregon Black History Project. Portland, Ore.: Georgian Press, 1980.

Mumford, Esther Hall. *Seattle's Black Victorians 1852–1901*. Seattle: Ananse Press, 1980.

Muscatine, Doris. *Old San Francisco: The Biography of a City from the Early Days to the Earthquake*. New York: G. P. Putnam's Sons, 1975.

Neville, Amelia Ransome. *The Fantastic City*. New York: Arno Press, 1975.

Papanikolas, Helen Z., ed. *The Peoples of Utah*. Salt Lake City: Utah State Historical Society, 1976.

Peavy, Linda, and Ursula Smith. *Pioneer Women: The Lives of Women on the Frontier*. Rowayton, Conn.: Saraband, 1996.

Pelz, Ruth. *Black Heroes of the Wild West.* Seattle: Open Hand Publishing, 1990.

Ploski, Harry A., and James Williams. *The Negro Almanac: A Reference Work on the African American.* Detroit: Gale Research, 1989.

Powell, Allan Kent, ed. *Utah History Encyclopedia: African Americans in Utah.* Salt Lake City: University of Utah Press, 1994.

Ravage, John W. *Black Pioneers: Images of the Black Experience on the North American Frontier.* Salt Lake City: University of Utah Press, 1997.

Reiter, Joan Swallow. *The Women: The Old West.* Alexandria, Va.: Time Life Books, 1978.

Savage, W. Sherman. *Blacks in the West.* Westport, Conn.: Greenwood Press, 1976.

Schlissel, Lillian. *Black Frontiers: A History of African American Heroes in the Old West.* New York: Simon & Schuster, 1995.

———. *Women's Diaries of the Westward Journey.* New York: Schocken Books, 1992.

Schrems, Suzanne H. *Uncommon Women, Unmarked Trails: The Courageous Journey of Catholic Missionary Sisters in Frontier Montana.* Norman, Okla.: Horse Creek Publications, 2003.

Smart, Donna Toland, ed. *Mormon Midwife: The 1846–1888 Diaries of Patty Bartlett Sessions.* Logan: Utah State University Press, 1997.

Smith, Barbara B., and Blythe Darlyn Thather, editors. *Heroines of the Restoration.* Salt Lake City: Bookcraft, 1997.

Smith, Jessie Carney. *Notable Black American Women.* Detroit: Gale Research, 1996.

———, ed. *Epic Lives: One Hundred Black Women Who Made a Difference.* Detroit: Visible Ink Press, 1993.

Sterling, Dorothy, ed. *We Are Your Sisters: Black Women in the Nineteenth Century.* New York: W. W. Norton, 1984.

Taylor, Quintard. *In Search of the Racial Frontier: African Americans in the American West 1528–1990.* New York: W. W. Norton, 1998.

Taylor, Quintard, and Shirley Ann Wilson Moore. *African American Women Confront the West 1600–2000.* Norman: University of Oklahoma Press, 2003.

Trachtman, Paul. *The Gunfighters: The Old West.* Alexandria, Va.: Time Life Books, 1974.

Turner, Erin H. *It Happened in Northern California.* Helena, Mont.: Falcon Publishing, 1999.

Whitley, Colleen. *Worth Their Salt: Notable but Often Unnoted Women of Utah.* Logan: Utah State University Press, 1996.

Wolfinger, Henry J. *A Test of Faith: Jane Elizabeth James and the Origins of the Utah Black Community.* New Canaan, Conn.: Readex, 1973.

The World's Congress of Representative Women, Vol. 1. Chicago: Rand McNally, 1894.

Magazines and Journals

"Bearden Exhibition Inspires Weekend Jazz Brunch at National Gallery's Terrace Café." National Gallery of Art [Landover, Md.] Press Release, September 14, 2003.

Bennett, Addison. "Woman Lives Century." *Oregonian* (August 24, 1924).

Bennett, Lerone Jr. "The Mystery of Mary Ellen Pleasant: Was She a Public Benefactor or a Public Menace? Part 1." *Ebony* (June 1993).

———. "The Mystery of Mary Ellen Pleasant—19th Century African-American Business Woman. Part 2." *Ebony* (September 1993).

Bentz, Donald N. *The Oracle* [AZ] *Historian,* summer 1982; winter 1984–85; summer 1983; spring 1988.

Bringhurst, Newell G. "The Mormons and Slavery—A Closer Look." *Pacific Historical Review* 50 (1981).

Brown, Philip S. "Old California Cook Books." *Book Club of California Quarterly News-Letter* 20:1 (1954).

Carroll, Lillian M. "Mary Fields." *Ohio Cues* (January 1977).

Cooper, Gary A. "Stagecoach Mary: Gun-toting Montanan Delivered U.S. Mail, as Told to Marc Crawford." *Ebony* (October 1959).

deGraaf, Lawrence B. "Race, Sex, and Region: Black Women in the West, 1850–1920." *Pacific Historical Review* 49 (May 1980).

Espich, Whitney T. "African American Women's History Savored through Exquisite Recipes." Radcliffe Institute for Advanced Study, Harvard Library (May 12, 2004).

Franks, James A. "Mary Fields: The Story of Black Mary." *Montana: The Magazine of Western History* (spring 2003).

Freeman, Judith. "Commemorating a L.A. Pioneer." *Angeles Magazine* (April 1990).

Green, Virginia. "Hidden Citizens: Blacks in Salem through the Years." *Historic Marion* [Marion County (OR) Historical Society] 40:1 (spring 2002).

Harris, Mark. "The Legend of Black Mary." *Negro Digest* (August 1950).

Hayes, Ralph, and Joe Franklin. "Northwest Black Pioneers: A Tribute." *Bon-Macys* (1994).

Katz, William Loren. "Pioneer Sisters' African American Frontier Women." *Essence* (February 1994).

Leishman, Nora. "Mechanics' Institute Fairs, 1857–1899." *Argonaut: Journal of the San Francisco Historical Society* (fall 1999).

Longone, Janice B. "Early Black-Authored American Cookbooks." *Gastronomica: The Journal of Food and Culture* (February 2001).

Nash, Sunny. "Mother Amadeus and Stagecoach Mary." *True West* 43:3 (March 1996).

Quarterly of the Oregon Historical Society 23:2 (June 1922).

Rattray, Diana. "What Mrs. Fisher Knows About Old Southern Cooking, Soups, Pickles, Preserves." *Southern U.S. Cuisine* (August 22, 1998).

Rowe, Monica Dyer. "What Mrs. Fisher Knows About Old Southern Cooking—Book Reviews." *American Visions* (August–September 1997).

Swyer, Sue. "The Legend of Stagecoach Mary." *Toledo Magazine, The Blade* (June 7, 1981).

"Women Set Type." *Social Design Notes* (April 14, 2004).

Young Woman's Journal: Organ of the Young Ladies' Mutual Improvement Associations 16 (1884).

Zafar, Rafia. "What Mrs. Fisher Knows About Old Southern Cooking." *Gastronomica: The Journal of Food and Culture* (fall 2001).

Newspapers

"California Portraits: Lydia Flood Jackson." *California Voice* (June 5, 1959).

Cayton, Susie Revels. "Tribulations of Wanters." *Seattle Republican* (January 19, 1900).

"Delilah Beasley, Trail Blazer." *Oakland Heritage Alliance News,* 8:4 (winter 1988–1989).

"Elizabeth Flood's School: Oakland's First African American Institution." *Oakland Heritage Alliance News* (winter 1992–1993).

"Ex-Slave Finds Long-Lost Daughter." *Colorado Prospector, Historical Highlights from Early Day Newspapers* (April 1970).

Fellow, Jill. "Jane Manning James—Black Pioneer." *Provo Daily Herald* (February, 16, 2005).

"Lydia Flood Jackson." *Knave, Oakland Tribune* (April 12, 1959).

"Lydia Flood Jackson Dies at 101." *San Francisco Chronicle* (July 7, 1963).

"Mary Fields Celebrates Her 83rd Birthday at Her Home in Cascade." *Cascade Courier* (March 16, 1913).

"Mary Sanderson and the Brooklyn School." *Oakland Heritage Alliance News* (winter–spring 1994).

"Mrs. Anna Neal Rites Are Set." *Tucson Daily Citizen* (May 12, 1950).

"Negro Centenarian Dies." *Oregonian* (January 27, 1925).

"'Nigger Mary' Fields, Early Day Resident of Cascade, One of State's Noted Characters." *Great Falls Tribune* (May 22, 1939).

"Oakland Briefing." *Oakland Heritage Alliance News* (summer 1994).

"Oldest Living City Native Observes 100th Birthday." *Oakland Tribune* (June 10, 1962).

"Old Timer Passes Away." *Cascade Courier* (December, 11, 1914).

"Rancher Remembers Mary Fields, Pioneer." *Great Falls Tribune* (April 18, 1975).

"Relic of Mammy Pleasant." *San Francisco Examiner* (October 10, 1964).

San Francisco Chronicle (August 12–15, 17, and 25, 1880).

Talwani, Sanjay. "Frontierswoman and Former Slave Was a Mission Character." *Great Falls Tribune* (January 30, 2000).

Tarbert, Jesse. "Horace Cayton 1859–1940." *Seattle Times* (March 1, 2004).

Tasker, Greg. "Hats Off to Mrs. Fisher, Her Recipes." *Detroit Free Press* (February 10, 2004).

Trahant, Mark. "Publisher Lost Paper to Prejudice." *West by Northwest Times* (October 8, 1998).

Other Sources

Balance Sheet for Mary E. Fields in Account with Ursuline Convent of the Sacred Heart. 1884–1885.

Berg, Peter, and Jane Arnold. *Feeding America: Exploring Historic Cookbooks at the MSU Library* (video). East Lansing: Michigan State University Press, 2004.

Burch, Pauline. *Pioneer Nathaniel Ford and the Negro Family.* Collection number Mss707. Oregon Historical Society Research Library Collections, Portland, 1953.

"Clara Brown, a Biography and Clara Brown's Colorado." Central City Opera Family Study Guide, Denver, 2003.

Easton-Black, Susan Ward. "Membership of the Church of Jesus Christ of Latter-day Saints" 29. Religious Studies Center, Brigham Young University, Utah, 1987 (unpublished compilation).

Great Register, Alameda County. April 15, 1877.

"Isaac Flood." Negroes Biography. Leonard Verbarg Papers, 1959.

Jensen, Andrew, compiler. "Journal History: A Collection of Early Sources." June 21, 1847.

John J. Pleasants, and Mary E., (his wife) Respondents vs. The North Beach and Mission Railroad Co., Appellant. Supreme Court of the State of California Brief for the Appellant, November 1867.

Lydia Flood Jackson funeral service card.

Lyman, Eliza. "Autobiography and Diary of Eliza Marie Partridge (Smith) Lyman 1820–1885." Held in L. Tom Perry Special Collections, copied by the Brigham Young University Library, 1945.

Lythgoe, Dennis Lee. "Negro Slavery in Utah." Thesis, University of Utah, 1966.

"Reminiscences of Mrs. Wm. Neal, Oracle," as told to Mrs. George F. Kitt, Arizona Historical Society.

Report of the Industrial Exhibition Under the Auspices of the Mechanics' Institute of the City of San Francisco 1878, 1879, 1880, 1881, and 1882.

St. Andrew's African Methodist Episcopal Church, Historical Statement, Sacramento.

St. Andrew's Church History, Sacramento.

U.S. Census records: 1870, 1880, 1900, and 1910.

"Woman Who Came to Oregon as Slave Spends Last Days in Home for Aged." Scrapbook 268, pp. 187–88. Oregon Historical Society Research Library Collections, Portland.

INDEX

About the Author

T RICIA MARTINEAU WAGNER, a North Carolina author and presenter, is an experienced elementary teacher and reading specialist. She is a well-versed and entertaining speaker who brings history to life. Wagner enjoys conducting presentations for schools and organizations around the country on the history of the Oregon Trail, African American women born before 1900, and the Underground Railroad, as well as creative writing for grades three through twelve.

Her other books include *It Happened on the Oregon Trail* and *It Happened on the Underground Railroad*. Wagner, an Ohio native, attended The University of Toledo and Miami University. An avid hiker in her free time, she makes her home in Charlotte with her husband, Mark; their children Kelsey and Mitch; and their puppy, Tiger. She can be reached at trishmwagner@earthlink.net.

Award-Winning TwoDot Titles

THE WOMEN WRITING THE WEST WILLA LITERARY AWARDS RECOGNIZE OUTSTANDING LITERATURE FEATURING WOMEN'S STORIES SET IN THE WEST.

2006 WINNER— MEMOIR/ESSAY

The Lady Rode Bucking Horses: The Story of Fannie Sperry Steele, Woman of the West
Dee Marvine

2006 FINALIST

Pioneer Doctor: The Story of a Woman's Work
Mari Graña

2006 FINALIST

More Than Petticoats: Remarkable Nevada Women
Jan Cleere

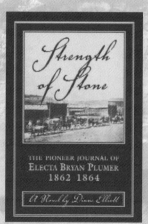

2003 FINALIST

Strength of Stone: The Pioneer Journal of Electa Bryan Plumer, 1862–1864
A Novel by Diane Elliott

Available wherever books are sold

Orders can be placed on the Web at www.GlobePequot.com, by phone at 1-800-243-0495, or by fax at 1-800-820-2329

TwoDot® is an imprint of The Globe Pequot Press

AFRICAN
AMERICAN
WOMEN
of the
OLD WEST